AF374821

THE 1,200 POUND TODDLER

THE INCREDIBLE HORSE

JANE SALKO

BEST LIFE BOOKS

I dedicate this book to my husband, Chris.
He knows why.

Contents

Author's Note

When I landed at Salko Farm with a bump, nothing in my life looked the way I thought it would. I wasn't broken, but I also wasn't exactly functioning. I was a fully grown adult woman with a résumé, responsibilities, and a nervous system that behaved like it had been raised by wolves and caffeinated toddlers.

I didn't come here seeking horses.

I came here seeking quiet.

Then, in the way the universe enjoys orchestrating plot twists, the horses found me first.

What happened next wasn't magical. It was biological.

My nervous system met their nervous systems, and suddenly all the things I'd been trying to out-think, out-run, or out-spiritualize... stopped hiding. Horses don't negotiate with your façade. They don't care about your titles or your coping strategies. They respond to who you are beneath all that. And for the first time in my life, I had to meet that person too.

This book came out of the moments when I was humbled, exposed, fascinated, and sometimes mildly embarrassed by just how accurate these 1,200-pound toddlers could be. It came out of a thousand small awakenings that added up to one giant truth: your body always knows what your mind has been trying to avoid.

The horses taught me presence. They taught me honesty. They taught me regulation, boundaries, trust, and the strange relief of letting go of a lifetime of subconscious tugs that never belonged to me. They held the mirror up, and whether I liked the reflection or not, they stayed right there beside me.

If you're picking up this book, chances are you're ready for that kind of mirror too.

Not the harsh one. Not the punishing one. The true one.

The one that shows you your brilliance and your buried calm.

The one that says, "You were never the problem. You were just unregulated."

My hope is that these pages help you breathe deeper, laugh harder, forgive faster, and maybe even grow up a little emotionally sooner than I did. And if any part of this helps you meet the version of yourself you've been circling for years, then every bump on the path to this farm was worth it.

Here's to presence.

Here's to freedom.

Here's to discovering your own inner peace, one nervous-system wobble at a time.

And here's to the horses who never stop telling the truth.

— **Jane**

INTRODUCTION

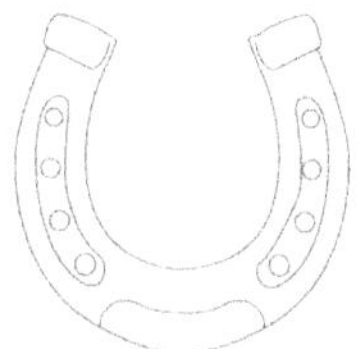

Horses.

What is it about horses that causes so many parents to nearly go broke trying to satisfy their child's desire for all things horse? Why does this obsession start at such a young age? I have researched this because the level of enchantment is extremely amazing.

This book has two purposes: To explain horses in as few words as possible to the parents of horse-obsessed children and to help both parent and child gain confidence on and around horses. I *was* this parent. I had zero knowledge of horses. My daughters rode and loved every single lesson and would never consider missing a ride. In the dead of winter—Horses. Steaming hot summer—Horses. Walking miles to pluck their horse for that lesson from a muddy field in the dark. Yep, horses.

At the time, I had too much of my own stuff going on, raising my four children, to learn more about these animals. I knew I wasn't comfortable around horses. I had zero interest in riding them or cleaning the sh*t off of them. Maybe I fed them a few carrots, with my eyes closed, praying that my fingers would remain attached to my hand. Otherwise, I didn't give horses much thought. When I look back now, that surprises me. I love to learn, but horses weren't on my radar. Not even with two mildly obsessed, extremely chatty daughters. I must have figured that there wasn't much point, as the amount you might need to know seemed intense, and I did not even consider having horses in my life at some later stage.

Fast-forward about twelve years, and I find myself living on a horse farm. This change was rather abrupt and all-encompassing. More will be revealed about how that transpired throughout this handy book.

A horse is basically a 1,200-pound toddler. They are authentic, true to themselves, erratic, simultaneously irritating and hilarious, all-in with emotion, non-conforming, with no care for the resulting effects on humans, charming, difficult, lovable, loud, quiet, and most of all, great judges of character.

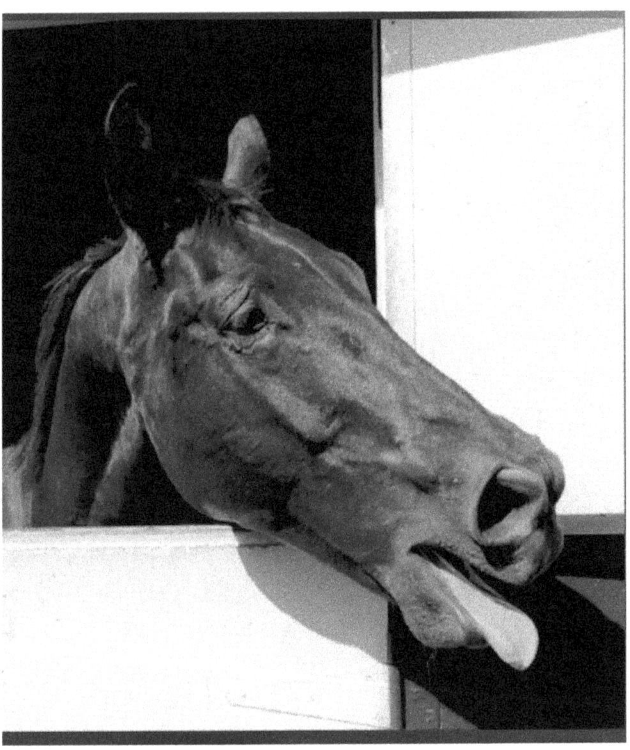

This may not make sense if you don't have a horse background, but it will by the end of this short book. You will suddenly appreciate the fact that your very own toddler—bless you if you are currently raising one—does not weigh 1,200 pounds.

CHAPTER 1

YOUR FIRST STEP INTO THE EQUESTRIAN WORLD

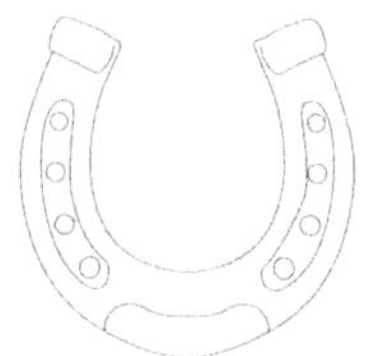

You're likely filled with anticipation, curiosity, and perhaps a dash of apprehension. After all, embarking on an equestrian journey is no small feat. Let me assure you that your decision to explore this path is exciting, promising countless rewards. Though having a full wallet isn't one of them.

The world of horses is vast and varied. From their majestic forms to their gentle spirits, these animals captivate hearts around the globe. You might not know that each horse carries its own unique personality; they are as individual and unique as humans are supposed to be.

Horses are often compared to toddlers due to their unfiltered expressiveness and seemingly untamed energy—imagine managing a 1,200-pound toddler.

This comparison might seem bizarre at first glance, but upon further exploration, it makes perfect sense. Just like toddlers exploring the world for the first time with wide-eyed wonder, horses, too, approach life with genuine curiosity and an unwavering spirit of adventure. They say, "Curiosity killed the cat"–they should have used the word "horse" instead. This curiosity begins on the day they are born and ends on the day they die. Any object is a potential hazard. I remember a specifically super scary day. You see, there was this December day that I naively took a terrifying new plant into the riding arena for Christmas. Yep, that 8-inch-tall poinsettia turned out to be the most terrifying thing to have ever entered the indoor arena.

This was an eye-opening day for me. It was beginning to sink in. I was starting to understand the level of consistency these horses needed in order to thrive.

In this book, we'll cover more than just their vibrant personalities; we will dive into understanding horses better: the lingo, therapeutic qualities, and practical information to consider when choosing a horse and training barn.

Horses are incredibly interesting and complex beings. Many of them seem perma-grouch like Oscar from Sesame Street but are usually softies once their innate fears subside. Only sometimes, though. Some horses are simply not meant to be handled by humans. An unruly and untrainable horse usually comes from some past trauma the horse has experienced at the hands of their past humans.

Horses talk primarily through body language—from flicks of their ears to movements of their tails—and every gesture carries meaning. The key is learning how to interpret these accurately, which will significantly enhance your relationship with them.

Understanding a horse's body language helps improve communication between rider and horse, effectively promoting mutual respect and trust. This is the most important aspect of the horse-human connection.

Scientific research also supports this claim. A study by Animal Behavior Consultants revealed that riders who took time to understand horse body language had stronger bonds with their equine companions than those who didn't.

In the words of Winston Churchill, "There is something about the outside of a horse that is good for the inside of a man." These beautiful creatures not only provide us with their strength and speed but also teach us lessons in patience, empathy, resilience, and authenticity.

Right here...   Right now.

Horses are right here, right now, all the time.

So, how can you foster this understanding? How can we learn lessons about authenticity from these nonverbal beings? It begins with spending time with horses, observing them in different scenarios—while they are grazing, playing with other horses, or even resting. Each observation offers insights into their behavior patterns, further aiding in decoding their body language.

Case studies from equine therapy sessions—specifically Equine Gestalt® and Touched by a Horse®, reveal remarkable transformations in individuals who spent regular time with horses. Individuals reported increased self-esteem, reduced anxiety levels, and an overall better mental health status post sessions. Visit the following website for scientific proof and more stories about the Equine Gestalt, personal stories of transformation, and other amazing things: https://touchedbyahorse.com/capstone-projects/

Spending quality time observing horse behavior greatly enhances your ability to understand them better. Understanding a horse better means you will also understand yourself better.

Fun Fact:

There is a distinct pecking order in any herd of horses. It is real, and when humans intervene with the order, things don't go well for the humans.

Points to Ponder:

• Horses use ears to express mood: forward-pointing ears indicate interest, while pinned-back ears signal anger. If you approach a horse and he pins his ears, step away from that horse. He is unhappy and is to be feared.

• Tail swishing could mean irritation or discomfort (or just an irritating fly).

• A lowered head often means a relaxed state, but it could show illness if it's too low. Horses will lower their heads right to the ground when in colic pain.

• Licking and chewing indicate relaxation.

• Horses make noises–they each mean a different thing. Refer to Equine Terminology for a more complete explanation.

• Pawing the ground with a front hoof usually means boredom and/or impatience. They will also paw at the snow to clear it away so they can reach the green grass below. When I first saw my horse, Paul, do that with the snow, I figured he was the smartest horsie ever... until I found out that they pretty much all do it.

• Different parts of a horse's body convey varied emotions; knowing what each movement means will significantly improve communication between you.

• Did you know that nearly 7 million people participate annually in horse-related activities in America? This speaks volumes about our deep-rooted fascination with these majestic animals.

• Horse riding isn't just an activity but a lifestyle choice that millions worldwide embrace passionately every day.

Now, let's walk through specific steps to start your family's equestrian journey.

1. Find a reputable trainer or riding school near you. (Chapter 16)

2. Start by taking horsemanship or beginner lessons on safety measures and basic riding techniques.

3. Spend time observing horses in their natural environment to understand their behavior better.

4. Regularly groom and care for a horse to build a strong bond.

5. Practice patience—remember, learning to ride is a gradual process;

rushing won't yield results. Ideally, two lessons per week is a great way to advance at a significant pace.

This book is about the 1,200-pound toddlers out there—yes, every horse on the planet fits into this book. Parents of horse-obsessed riders need to read this book to best understand the benefits, investment, challenges, and wonder of equine involvement. Understanding more about the magic of horses and your little darlin's obsessions goes a long way.

Now, let's talk about horse obsession, shall we?

CHAPTER 2

FROM FAIRY TALES TO FIELDS: UNRAVELING THE EQUINE FASCINATION

Why does every little girl seem obsessed with horses? And plenty of little boys, too! This phenomenon transcends cultures and generations, persisting even in today's digital age. This chapter uncovers the roots of this fascination, dives deeply into equine history, and explores how our relationship with these majestic creatures reflects upon us as humans.

Horses have been intertwined with human history since time immemorial. They've served as a means of transportation, symbols of wealth and power, companions in battle, and even deities in certain cultures. Interestingly enough, despite their well-documented historical significance—from cave paintings to classical literature—we rarely stop to consider their impact on our personal lives or psyche.

The horse's evolution is just as captivating as its role in human society. Starting from *Eohippus*, a small creature about the size of a fox, they evolved over 55 million years into what we now know as *Equus*: an animal characterized by gracefulness and strength. This journey mirrors man's own evolution path; perhaps that's one reason we feel such a deep connection.

Now, let's explore why these animals captivate us so much. At our farm, we see mainly girls between the ages of 4 and 12 who seem to develop an almost inexplicable bond with horses. Having said that, it's been my experience that horses enhance the lives of people of all ages. Horses are often associated with freedom and adventure—themes prevalent in many children's fairy tales and books featuring horses, like *Black Beauty* or *The Secret Horse.*

Moreover, interacting with horses allows children to engage all five senses simultaneously, a rare experience in today's screen-dominated world, which can be both stimulating and soothing. There is also evidence that nurturing relationships with animals fosters empathy during developmental years; hence, another reason for this profound equine love. And how about intuition and the increased access to this sixth sense, especially in the presence of horses? All of this is also true for adults. Horses inherently encourage somatic experiences.

For example, a study conducted by the Cummings School of Veterinary Medicine at Tufts University found that children involved in equestrian activities were less anxious and had better overall mental health than their peers. Countless scientific studies have been performed over the past four-plus decades, all pointing toward improved mood and productivity after time spent with horses. **Hope** is another frequently used word post-Equine Gestalt session.

Analyzing this equine fascination further reveals it to be more than just an innocent childhood obsession; it's actually a potent tool for personal growth and development. The lessons learned from caring for these animals can shape your values, resilience, and character. What a fabulous understatement that is.

Consider the meaning of values. If sound decision-making is your goal in life, core values are required. People are not able to comfortably make well-informed decisions without consciously knowing their top five core values. Horses are often used in rehabilitation programs with wonderfully positive and scientifically backed outcomes. There is a ranch in Pennsylvania that has success rates in the 90% + level with suicide attempt reintegration into society after time spent at this ranch.

Consider the case of Molly, a 9-year-old girl who participated in a therapeutic horsemanship program after her parents' divorce. Despite her initial fear and reluctance, she gradually grew confident around horses. Her self-esteem soared as she learned how to groom, feed, and ride them. This newfound confidence spilled over into other areas of her life as well.

Interactions with horses can and will foster personal growth and development in children. All children who spend quality time with horses experience an overt and healthy softening.

———

Fun Facts:

• Horses have been domesticated for over 5,000 years.

• *Equus* is Latin for "horse."

• Girls between the ages of 7 and 11 are most likely to show interest in horses. And when they do, you might as well set fire to your wallet and kiss any new adult clothing goodbye! The upside, though–the house is quiet while the girls are "at the barn." The joke about the clothing, though, is no joke, sorry.

Equine obsession often peaks during middle childhood but can continue into adulthood. We have adult riders at Salko Farm. Some are brand new to riding, while others are returning after taking a break for many decades. Regardless of whether they are seasoned or a newbie, they do *not* like to miss their weekly or twice-weekly rides.

According to a survey from American Horse Publications (AHP), there are about two million horse owners in America alone, with about *seventy percent being female*. This data shows us that the love affair with horses extends far beyond childhood fantasies; it's truly an enduring bond running deep within our collective psyche.

Points to Ponder:

The fascination with horses isn't just limited to children; it also stays prevalent among adults—*especially women*.

To nurture this passion further or even rekindle your own equine love affair, consider taking the following steps:

• Visit a local stable: Get up close and personal with these magnificent creatures. Offer to volunteer.

• Enroll in horse riding lessons: This can be an exciting way to get fit and learn new skills. Horseback riding is a technical sport, ideal for A-type achievers who love a challenge.

• Read equestrian literature: Works of Anna Sewell, Joe Camp, Monty Roberts, Melisa Pearce, or Walter Farley are great starting points. *Centered Riding* by Sally Swift is really the best place to start if you are interested in riding. Sally Swift provides riders with a solid foundation. With these foundations in your toolbox, you can participate in any of the various events or styles of equestrian sport.

• Watch horse-themed movies/TV Shows: *Spirit* or *Heartland*, a great Canadian show, might just reignite your passion for horses.

Remember, it's never too late to embark on this equine journey—whether you're a little girl dreaming of galloping unicorns or an adult yearning for some therapeutic trotting in the countryside!

CHAPTER 3

THE EXTENSIVE BENEFITS OF SPENDING TIME WITH HORSES FOR CHILDREN AND TEENS

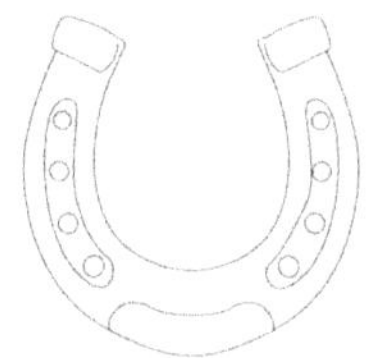

Hold Your Horses 🐴

With the number of teen suicides reaching all-time highs, especially in the Northeast of the USA, it is more and more essential that we begin to look at the possibilities of having groups of school kids spend some "slow down time" with horses. Horses have long been revered for their grace, power, and beauty, but what may surprise many is the profoundly positive impact they can have on the emotional, social, and physical development of children and teens. This is so important, I would like to say it again: Horses *will* profoundly and positively impact the emotional, social, and physical development of your children and teens.

Whether through horseback riding, caring for horses, or simply spending time with them in a therapeutic environment, horses offer a wide array of benefits that contribute to the well-being and growth of young people. Growth in emotional intelligence and self-esteem happens by osmosis. Kids will improve their physical fitness and begin to learn real-life responsibility. The incredible bond between children and horses is a powerful force for positive change, is organic, and easily facilitates reductions in anxiety levels.

I have seen firsthand the obvious signs of reduced anxiety levels in most children who have simply placed a single hand on a horse.

Enhancing Somatic Connection | Building Emotional Intelligence

Spending time with horses offers an exceptional opportunity for children and teens to develop emotional intelligence. Horses are highly sensitive animals that respond to a person's mood and emotions, often mirroring or reacting to how they are treated or even to what they are speaking and feeling. This sensitivity can help young people become more attuned to their own emotions as well as to the emotions of others. Here are some ways we see emotional intelligence develop in kids as a result of time spent with horses.

- **Self-Awareness:** Interacting with a horse requires a young person to be mindful of their own feelings and body language. Horses react to subtle cues like tension, frustration, or calmness, encouraging children and teens to reflect on how they feel and learn to regulate their emotions. Horses can tell whether a human is congruent from up to 30 feet away.
- **Empathy:** As young people spend time with horses, they begin to understand the animal's emotions and needs. Horses communicate through body language and non-verbal cues, teaching children to recognize and interpret signals beyond words. This can deepen their empathy, helping them to connect better with others in their lives.
- **Special Somatic Connection:** The physical presence and movement of the horse will most certainly create somatic resonance within the child. This allows them to feel and connect with the horse's energy and rhythms. Overall, the increase in somatic awareness is the most natural occurrence when you combine horses with humans. The increased awareness in humans allows for better regulation of emotions as they arise. Yet another level of awareness will undoubtedly unfold as we begin to understand how wonderful and important it is for us to slow down and tune in to all of our senses and our bodies in wholeness.
- **Patience and Resilience:** Horses are not always easy to control or understand. Building trust with a horse takes time, patience, and consistent effort. Children and teens learn the

importance of perseverance, delayed gratification, and managing frustration when things don't go as planned. With horses, this is not only a possibility, it is most likely. With many horses, with their... let's call them *interesting* traits and characteristics, MANY things will NOT go as planned. Horses hopefully teach children that to be embarrassed or to look vulnerable or "new" is simply a part of life. The more you do it, the easier it gets. Horses allow children to not take themselves so seriously. ✌ As an aside here, and one of the reasons for this book, many of today's parents, especially in the more powerful and populated cities like NY, Chicago, and Dallas, inadvertently provide a pressure-filled context of life. Kids pick up on this—it may be nothing you actually say to them; it's simply the constant stress and overwhelm they observe within the family unit.

I will share an example of the pressure local children at our farm have faced. Situation: A Sunday Schooling Horse Show at Salko Farm. Schooling shows are super low-key and family-oriented; come watch Little Suzie ride and grab a ribbon. It's a nice day. We are running behind, and a father looks at his watch and exclaims to the wife (though all children present were included in the "conversation)—"Well, if we had known they were going to be running so far behind, we could have taken her to soccer practice first!" Horseback riding is physical—and isn't one pressure-filled event per day enough?

Enhancing Self-Esteem and Confidence

The relationship between a young person and a horse can be deeply empowering. Horses are large and unpredictable, and yet, when properly handled, they offer young people the opportunity to take charge of something bigger than themselves. I don't know about you, but one of the sweetest things in the world that I have had the pleasure to experience is watching a tiny child horse-lover, not even three feet tall, leading her very own 1,200-pound "toddler" to the barns.

The challenges involved in caring for and riding horses can significantly boost a child or teen's confidence. This enhances self-worth and allows for a better understanding of themselves and how they show up in this world. In a world full of confusion and instability, the more sure anyone is of their vision for their future, the more overall clarity of self and direction they will experience. This is a huge topic of mine so I will further address this here and now. Any person without a vision for their future is simply at the mercy of others (parents, coaches, bosses), as well as the media and all its suggestions. No vision means your mind has more wide open potential to be led off in any direction towards any seemingly new and shiny object or procedure, exercise, or specific food or supplement that will fix or help you.

No vision with your must-haves for your future leaves you less protected against the media and peer pressure when you are younger. The more solid a child's sense of self is, and the sense of feeling worthy within their own family, the better standing they possess when it comes to vision and keeping the media suggestions at bay.

Sense of Accomplishment: Learning to ride or care for a horse involves developing skills that take time and practice. Whether it's grooming a horse, leading it, or mastering the art of riding, each small success builds more and more confidence. Doing one thing that scares you every single day—like being in the presence of horses. For many young people, riding a horse for the first time or successfully navigating an obstacle course can provide a tremendous sense of achievement, especially if past fear of horses, or similar, has kept one away from them. These things provide surprisingly high levels of achievement and joy in adults leading horses, too! It amazes me that I continue to be filled with joy every time I witness anyone reaching out to touch a horse for the very first time.

Responsibility: Horses require a great deal of care, from feeding and grooming to mucking out stalls and ensuring their overall well-being. When you've been around horses long enough, you learn to see signs of colic in the way the bedding looks in any particular stall. They are incredibly readable to a human who has spent decent amounts of time with these incredibly somatic and intuitive creatures.

Taking responsibility for the care of an animal can instill a strong sense of duty, which in turn boosts self-esteem. The commitment involved in looking after a horse fosters maturity and reliability. At our farm, kids are given a lot of responsibility at quite young ages. They shadow other older grooms for several months until they show the instructors that they have the maturity and confidence to have a horse groomed and tacked correctly and in the riding arena (the ring) just five minutes prior to the lesson.

Factors Involved In Grooming and Tacking a Horse:

If a person has been taught well, they will know the purpose and timing of each tool and the reason we use it for grooming. For example, the curry comb. It's usually a round or oval shape with many nubs or teeth in several round or oval rows. The purpose is to raise the dirt to the surface so that a hard brush can sweep the dirt away. I ask the little kids if they would like to have the sand out of their bathing suits after a day at the beach and before they ride home in the car. They say yes (hopefully) and understand that a horse doesn't need to have sand rubbing his skin under the saddle any more than they need that on their way home. The soft brush follows the hard brush. If they are shod with shoes, you need to pick the hooves to check for wedged stones or damage to the hooves or shoes.

Tacking includes saddle type and size; there are many variations of both available. Saddles also have different lengths of billet straps and different types of trees. There is a girth size, a saddle pad, and some horses require a bumper pad (extra cushioning) between the saddle and the saddle pad. Other items of tack are listed at the beginning of this book.

Overcoming Fear: Horses, with their size and power, can be intimidating at first. However, overcoming the initial fears of riding or handling them teaches young people how to manage anxiety and tackle challenges head-on. The sense of triumph that comes from facing those fears directly can create lasting feelings of self-worth. Doing one thing daily that scares you sure is character-building!

As a silly aside from 2005, we had just moved our family of six from London, England, to Ontario, Canada. I was 39 years old and grossly overweight. My youngest child was two years old, so I felt a little lame whenever I found myself saying it was baby weight. A friend from high school convinced me to join an indoor soccer team of 40+ women, but she couldn't be there on my first night. How bad could going alone be?

So on that rainy and foggy evening, I drove myself down to Oakville, Ontario, from Milton—approximately 16 miles. My friend wasn't there for moral support, and I didn't know another soul in attendance. Let's add that I had never played indoor soccer, and it was insanely more difficult and faster-paced than I could have imagined. Outdoor soccer seemed like a cakewalk in comparison. I slowly, and with much resistance, allowed myself to remember that it had been more than two *decades* since I had played an actual game of soccer. Anyway, in indoor soccer, you can use the sideboards to bounce the ball off as you zoom around your opponent. Yes, wildness. Also, there is barely any stopping. In the first five minutes of waddling around the small pitch, I was entirely exhausted, seeing little white starry lights, and my face was the color of beets.

The ref asked me if I was okay. I declared that "I was fine!" though it took me at least 20 seconds to tell him. Vulnerability is real. It is a thing that most people, especially adults, avoid like the plague. To look like you are "new" to something can stop us from trying absolutely anything and everything new.

That night, I said to myself out loud in the car on my way to that initial middle-aged women's indoor soccer game, "I am supposed to do one thing that scares me every single day. This one thing on this day gets me off that hook for at least one whole week!" Spending a "scary" day with horses is *way* easier.

Stress Reduction: Physical activities like horseback riding contribute to stress reduction. Exercise generally promotes the release of endorphins—natural chemicals in the brain that help improve mood. In addition, spending time outdoors and interacting with horses can serve as a calming activity, especially for children and teens who may experience stress from school, social pressures, family pressures, or other sources. In this life, there are not enough opportunities to enjoy structured, efficient downtime (though efficient downtime seems like an oxymoron). No over-thinking. No screens. No talking.

Developing Social Skills

Horses are not just an individual endeavor; they also encourage collaboration and communication. Children and teens often work together in equine programs, whether caring for horses, riding in groups, or competing. At Salko Farm, we see kids of various ages mixing together. Social restraints or differences are less obvious, almost non-existent, near horses. We frequently see fourth to ninth-grade girls gathered in groups.

Teamwork: In group riding lessons or EAS programs, young people often work together to solve problems and support one another. Whether it's preparing horses for riding or coordinating during group activities, teamwork and open communication are keys to success. These shared experiences create bonds among peers and foster a sense of community—something lacking in and around the larger cities of the world.

Communication Skills: Horses require clear, calm communication. Young people must learn to give commands in a way the horse can understand, which leads to better communication with people. They also develop the ability to listen to the horse's responses and instructions from instructors, mentors, or peers. Everyone needs to be on the same page when horses are involved. Mistakes can be costly and inconvenient.

Social Confidence: Participating in equine-related activities can help young people develop the confidence to socialize with others. Whether taking lessons at a stable, participating in a 4-H club, or competing in horse shows, being involved in the equine community encourages positive social interactions and helps build lasting friendships. Even the need for louder voices around horses provides an opportunity for growth and healing. Some children are afraid to raise their voices due to past trauma or timidity. Horses help with this consciously facilitated volume adjustment, showing that not every loud voice is to cause harm, but to create safety.

Therapeutic Benefits and Emotional Healing.

Equine Assisted Services are increasingly recognized as an effective form of therapy for children and teens dealing with a variety of emotional, mental, and physical challenges. The nonjudgmental nature of horses and their calming presence make them ideal partners in therapeutic settings. My horse, Paul, is drawn to more "broken" people. The more troubled the child, teen, or adult, the more in contact Paul remains, with complete connection and focus.

Emotional Healing: Trauma is a part of everyone's life. Most recently, children who experienced COVID and all that meant within the context of their little (and often confusing) family lives. For children and teens who have experienced trauma, loss, or mental health struggles, horses can provide a safe and supportive outlet for emotional healing. Many of my younger clients will say something out loud for the first time to my wonder horse, Paul. Sharing a secret will decrease the burden of that secret, even if it is only shared with an equine. Grooming, leading, or riding a horse can help release pent-up emotions and offer a sense of peace. This goes for any human.

Autism and ADHD Support: Equine Assisted Services have been shown to benefit children with autism, ADHD, and other developmental disorders. The rhythm of the horse's gait can have a soothing effect, while the sensory experience of interacting with the horse helps improve focus and emotional regulation. Horses do have the energetic ability to help humans rebalance and regulate. As I've said many times, the relationship built with a horse can increase a child's social skills and confidence. One can feel the peace a horse offers from a distance as they match our biorhythms and do their best to help slow our heart rates down. Shoulders will lower and relax. People may even shudder, yawn, or sigh. More on this in Chapter 10.

Anger Management: Working with horses requires patience and calmness, which can be particularly beneficial for teens struggling with anger issues. A horse's sensitivity to human emotions means they respond quickly to tense, aggressive behaviors, providing an immediate feedback loop for young people to adjust their attitudes and actions. A horse will do its best to remind a person to breathe, slowing down its breath in the hopes that the human will follow suit. This allows for that much-needed peace of mind.

Encouraging a Connection to Nature: Horses are often kept in rural or farm settings, allowing children and teens to connect with the outdoors. This connection to nature is essential for their development, providing mental and physical benefits. We do our best to discourage cellphone use while at the farm. Disconnection from the big bad world becomes a huge part of their most peaceful moments each week.

Environmental Awareness: Increased somatic awareness is a massive benefit of outdoor experiences. Breathing some fresh air, hearing the birds and the wind in the trees—spending time with horses in natural settings can foster a sense of environmental stewardship and a deeper respect for animals and the land. This connection to nature can also help alleviate the pressures of modern life, offering a sense of calm and perspective. Look into The Earthing Movie for more nature tips.

Decreased Screen Time: Children and teens are increasingly connected to technology; spending time outdoors with horses provides a healthy alternative to screen time. Spending time in nature, away from the distractions of phones and digital devices, can enhance mental clarity and focus. Less phone and more horse and eye contact with others are all mantras at Salko Farm.

The benefits of spending time with horses for children and teens extend far beyond learning to ride and any words I could "magic" onto the paper. From emotional growth and social development to physical health and therapeutic healing, horses offer young people a unique and multifaceted avenue for personal growth and development. The lessons these kids learn from being near these incredible creatures are too many to list. They quickly find huge amounts of responsibility, patience, empathy, and resilience. They find that slowing down and being more present allows for a quieter mind and maybe even a fresh perspective. This, in turn, enables them natural access to the most authentic versions of themselves. In an increasingly fast-paced and digital world, horses provide an enduring reminder of the power of connection to other living beings and the natural world. This is an area very close to my heart. Humans need to slow down, disconnect, and start learning to feel the feels as they organically begin to surface.

Connection with others is one of the primary needs of humans. For many people, connection with other humans is more complex than we imagined. A horse allows for an experience of connection.

Horses are right here, right now. They are like that *all* the time. If humans could be present even 50% of the time, the world would be a better place. Ninety to ninety-five percent of the time, we are technically "awake," but we are actually in our subconscious minds. We are only fully aware (conscious) of what we are doing for an average of 5-10% of any day. Our subconscious minds are not exactly current, and often store information incorrectly. This tells me that there isn't a lot of potential for clear thought and sensible actions... we are mostly "blind" on autopilot. Please think about that again for a minute. It really is the ticket to substantial change in the world—if people were present more of the time, there would be much less neurosis.

Suppose humans could spend more time being conscious, questioning all their old, automatic, and out-of-date responses to everything. Doesn't it make sense that we would be more relevant, relatable, balanced, and happy?

CHAPTER 4

THE EQUESTRIAN LINGO– DEMYSTIFYING HORSE TERMINOLOGY FOR PARENTS

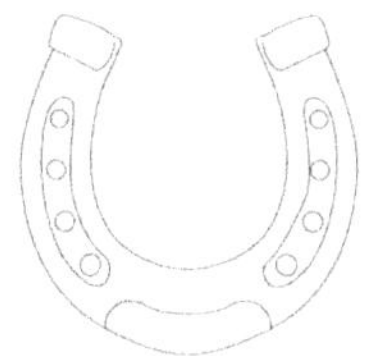

When your child comes home from the barn spouting phrases like, "gate shy," "more whoa than go," and "more leg," you might feel as if you've entirely missed the fact that your child is now bilingual, and it happened pretty much overnight. Welcome to the world of horse terminology. This chapter will guide you through this equestrian jargon, enabling you to understand what your kids are talking about and even join in on their conversations.

Let's begin our adventure into the world of horse lingo with short, easy-to-understand explanations.

1. Lameness: This term refers to when a horse has difficulty moving because of an injury or illness. It's equivalent to limping in humans.

2. Gate Shy: A "gate-shy" horse is one that hesitates or refuses to go through gates—similar to how some people have a fear of confined spaces. It can also mean that every time they pass the gate of the arena, they try to exit. For the visual, this means that the horse takes an unexpected 90 degree turn to the left or right, unbeknownst to the rider (sans seatbelt) on top of the feisty 1,200-pound Toddler. Rider eats the dirt.

3. More Whoa Than Go: If your child says their pony is "more whoa than go," it means the pony prefers slowing down (whoa) over speeding up (go). In other words, it's a lazy horse.

4. In Your Pocket: An "in your pocket" horse loves human attention and tends to follow people around just like a keen puppy would. Extroverted and happy to greet you.

5. Loosen the Reins/Tighten the Girth/Cinch: These are instructions related to riding equipment; loosening the reins gives the horse more freedom, while tightening the girth (the strap that keeps the saddle in place) ensures security during a ride. A loose girth could result in the saddle, with the rider attached, slipping right around and under the belly of the horse. You can't even imagine how tangled and messy that looks, never mind all the obvious reasons you wouldn't want to try that at home.

Key Idea:

Understanding equestrian lingo can help bridge communication gaps between you and your child, fostering better understanding and shared interests.

As Albert Einstein aptly put it, "If you can't explain it simply, you don't understand it well enough." In decoding these terms for you, we hope to make the world of horses a little simpler and far more accessible.

Let's look at how you can solve some common problems using your newfound knowledge. If your child complains about a gate shy horse, suggest they try introducing the horse to the gate slowly, allowing it to sniff and familiarize itself with this new object. They will pick up phrases during a lesson or while hanging out at the barn, and may not yet know quite what it means, so if you know something (imagine that, she might think you know something!) she learns and your connection with her strengthens.

On the other hand, if their pony is more whoa than go, perhaps they need to use stronger leg cues or consult their riding instructor for extra training tips. Sometimes carrying a crop is all it takes to let the horse know that you may in fact use it to quicken up the pace.

In scenarios where problems persist or seem severe, like lameness, it's best to involve a professional like a veterinarian or an experienced horse trainer. They have specialized knowledge that can provide suitable solutions.

Now, let's address a misconception. Many people mistakenly believe that tightening the girth means making it as tight as possible. This is not necessarily true, as over-tightening can cause discomfort or even injury. The girth should be secure but not overly restrictive. Think snug, not suffocating.

Points to Ponder:

• Lameness refers to difficulty in movement because of injury or illness.

• A gate-shy horse hesitates or refuses near gates.

• More whoa than go shows a lazy horse.

• An in-your-pocket horse loves attention and follows people around.

• Loosening reins gives the horse freedom; tightening girth ensures saddle security during rides.

Remember: Understanding equals connection. By understanding equestrian lingo, you're connecting with your child's passion and creating shared experiences that strengthen your bond while expanding your own horizons into this fascinating world of equine endeavor. Kids pay attention when horses are in the picture. To have any children in this era actually show interest in something that doesn't involve phones and does involve large sentient beings is amazing and should be capitalized upon if you are able to. The true extent of the secret benefits of these authentic and soulful creatures is yet to be determined. We already know more about the horse-human connection than I'm sure anyone ever thought possible. The depth and breadth of this knowledge grow every single day, globally.

In the next chapter, we'll cover the bulk of equestrian terminology.

CHAPTER 5

EQUINE TERMINOLOGY

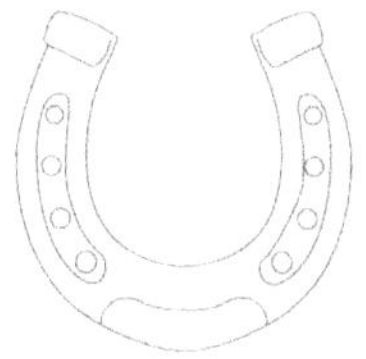

Now that you've got some of the equestrian lingo demystified, let's hop into general terminology. This will help you throughout the book and in any of your equestrian conversations.

ACTION: The way a horse moves

AIDS: Signals given to the horse with hands, voice, legs, and weight—also crops and spurs

APPALOOSA: A breed of horse and a color of horse

APPY: Short for Appaloosa

ARAB: Short for Arabian

ARABIAN: A breed of horse–known to be a little bit uppity or "salty" as the younger crowd says. I seriously never thought I would ever, ever use that expression. Sigh 😊

AT GRASS: A horse that is pastured year-round; one source of nutrition is grass

BALK: When a horse refuses to move or do what the rider wants

BARREL: The horse's midsection—a big, round barrel is sometimes harder to ride

BARREL RACE: A rodeo event where the horse is raced around three barrels and is timed. It's only open to females, and they are the coolest chicks on the planet! Just ask Kitty -

BAY: A chestnut or sorrel horse with black legs and tail, or a brown body with black legs and tail

BIT: The metal part of the bridle that goes in the horse's mouth

BLAZE: A wide white marking that goes down the face

BLUE ROAN: A black horse with speckled white hairs

BOX TO: To lead a horse up the ramp and into a horse box or trailer

BREAK: The act of training or gentling a horse

BREED: A particular type of horse

BREAST COLLAR: A leather piece of tack that goes across the horse's chest, helping to keep the saddle in place or just to be decorative

BRIDLE: The piece of tack that goes on the horse's head and is used to help control the horse

BROKEN-IN: A horse that can be ridden and handled

BRONCO: A horse that works in the rodeo, bucking off cowboys

BROOD MARE: A female horse kept for breeding

BUCK: When a horse kicks its hind legs into the air with its front legs on the ground, usually out of joy

CANTER: The three-beat gait that is faster than the trot and slower than the gallop

CANTLE: Back part of the saddle seat

CHAFF: Finely chopped hay used to add bulk to the feed

CHESTNUT: A color type where the horse has a reddish brown body, mane, and tail

CINCH (Also known as a GIRTH in English Riding Circles): The strap that goes around the horse's midsection to hold the saddle on

COLT: A male horse under four years old

CONCUSSION: Continuous banging of the horse's feet on hard ground

CONDITION: A horse's overall health and fitness

CONFORMATION: The way a horse's body is put together

CORONET BAND: Where the hoof meets the hair on the leg

CREST: Along the top of the horse's neck, where the mane grows

CRIBBING: When a horse grabs onto something, usually a fence or stall, and swallows air. It is a bad habit that is hard to correct. Cribbing is mentally addictive and learned from other horses that crib.

CROP: A short riding whip

CRUPPER: A piece of leather under the tail to keep the saddle from sliding forward

CUTTING HORSE: A horse trained to "cut" one calf out of a herd and keep it separate

DAM: A mother horse

DAPPLE: Circular markings found most often on grays

DEWORMER: Used to kill worms in horses

DOCK: The part of the tail that is bone

DORSAL STRIPE: A black stripe down the back of the horse

DRAFT: A large, slow type of workhorse used for pulling loads—examples are Shires and Belgians, Clydesdales too

DRESSAGE: A style of riding where horse and rider perform movements with time and precision

DUN: A yellowish coat color with a dorsal stripe down the back

ENGLISH: A style of riding

EQUINE: A horse, or having to do with horses

EQUESTRIAN: Someone who rides or interacts with horses

EQUINE GESTALT: A somatic-psychology practitioner who utilizes horse-human attunement and the principles of Gestalt theory to facilitate present-moment awareness, emotional integration, and resolution of unfinished patterns

EQUUS CABALLUS: The scientific name for horse

EVENTING: A competition involving three disciplines of dressage, cross-country, and show jumping

FARRIER: A horseshoer/blacksmith

FETLOCK: The joint between the knee and hoof

FEATHER: The tuft of hair on the horse's fetlock

FENDER: The area above the stirrup on Western saddles

FILLY: A female horse under four years old

FILL IN: A horse who knows what you are asking for and fills in–even if your "asks" are ambiguous as an inexperienced rider

FLY SPRAY: Insecticide used to kill or repel flies

FLYING LEAD CHANGE: When a cantering horse changes leads without breaking gait

FOAL: A baby horse

FROG: The V-shaped part of the horse's foot, which acts as a shock absorber

GAITS: The different ways that horses travel–The main gaits are walk, trot, canter, and gallop

GAITED HORSE: A horse that is either born or trained to do gaits other than the four regular ones. Some gaited horses do these naturally; others need chains, weights, and other devices to produce them, such as "big lick" walkers

GASKIN: The muscle above the hock in the horse's hind leg

GALLOP: The fastest of the equine gaits

GELDING: A neutered male horse (also the act of neutering a horse)

GIRTH: Another name for the cinch, usually used by English riders

GROOM: The act of cleaning a horse. n. A person who grooms and cares for horses

GYMKHANA: An event or show that consists of games on horseback —arena races, egg-in-spoon races, musical chairs, and barrel racing are some examples

HACKAMORE: A bitless bridle that works on the horse's nose and chin

HAND: A unit of 10 cm (4 in) used to measure the height of a horse. Horse height is measured at the highest point of the withers

HAY NET: A loosely woven rope bag made to hold hay

HOCKS: The joint in the hind legs of a horse between the knee and the fetlock, the angle of which points backward

HOOF PICK: A metal implement used to remove mud and stones from a horse's hooves

HORN: A part of the saddle

IRONS: Stirrup irons are attached to the saddle and designed to support the rider's feet; English stirrups

JOG: A slow trot

JOHDPURS: Stretchy English pants

JOCKEY: A very small, strong, and light person who rides racehorses

LIGHT HORSE: A type of horse used for riding and driving, not for pulling loads

LEAD ROPE: A rope used to lead and tie horses

LEADING REIN: Inside rein

LOPE: A slow, Western-style canter

LOSE A STIRRUP: When you drop your stirrup while riding, riding is tricky without stirrups

LOUNGE: Exercising a horse on the end of a lounge line

MARE: A female horse over four years old

MANURE: What you muck out of the stall (horse poop!)

MUCKING OUT: Cleaning stalls

NAVICULAR BONE: A small bone in the hoof, just behind the coffin bone

NAVICULAR DISEASE: A disease that disintegrates the navicular bone

NEARSIDE: The left-hand side of a horse

OFFSIDE: The right-hand side of a horse

OTTB: An 'off the track' thoroughbred horse means the horse has done some racing at the track

PAINT: A breed of horse that usually has pinto coloration—some solids do occur

PALOMINO: A coat color of tan body and white mane and tail. Barbie's original horse was a Palomino

PINTO: A coat pattern with large blotches of white and black or another color over the body—any breed may be a pinto

PLEASURE RIDING: Riding for pleasure, not showing

POLL: The highest point of the horse, located between the ears

PONY: Horse under 14.2 hands

QUARTER HORSE: A breed of horse

RACING: An event where horses run to see which is the fastest

REINING: A Western event

ROPING: A Western event where a calf is roped

ROUND PEN: A circular pen used to exercise or train horses

SADDLE: A padded and usually leather seat used to ride a horse

SADDLEBRED: A breed of horse

SHOWING: Competing for money, ribbons, or points with horses

STALLION: A male horse over four that has not been gelded

STUD: A male horse used for breeding

TACK: Equipment used to ride and train horses

TENNESSEE WALKER: A breed of horse, usually gaited

THOROUGHBRED: A breed of horse

TRANSITION: A change in gait

TURN IN: To bring the horses in from the pasture

TURN OUT: To put a horse out to pasture

VICE: Any bad habit a horse may have

WARM BLOOD: A breed of horse

WELSH PONY: A breed of pony

WORMS: Parasites that can injure or kill horses

XENOPHON: A Greek man known as "The Father of Classical Equitation" (430-ca 335 B.C.); he wrote the first fully preserved manual on the care of the riding horse: *The Art of Horsemanship.*

YEARLING: A horse that is one year old

ZEBRA MARKS: Stripes on the legs, withers, neck, or rump of some primitive breeds

Harley

CHAPTER 6

A HORSE IS A TODDLER? THE UNSPOKEN CONNECTION

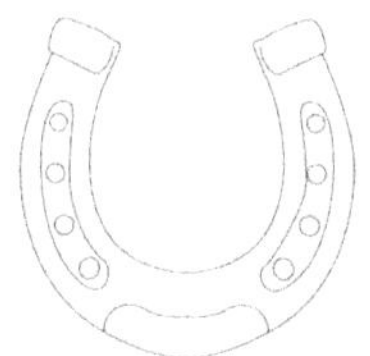

Imagine having a toddler. Now, picture that toddler weighing around 1,200 pounds and possessing the power to run at high speeds. Yes, we're talking about horses—your child's new best friend or perhaps yours. To understand the nuances of horse management and riding, it's essential to grasp this fundamental concept: horses are akin to toddlers. Take a second to let this information settle in... it really is useful information.

What you see is what you get when you look into the innocent eyes of your equine companion. There are no hidden masks; their feelings are as clear as daylight. Just like toddlers express their fear through tears or fits, horses exhibit their fright through snorting or erratic movements (spooks). This is often experienced as suddenly realizing you are on the ground with dirty breeches and bright red cheeks. If you are in an age category similar to mine—i.e., as old as the hills—there is a much-needed "broken bone check" that needs to happen before you get back up on an oblivious horse with your bright red cheeks. Vulnerability is real where horses are concerned, and let me tell you, that is magic in itself for the humans.

Why does this happen?

The answer comes from instinctive behavior patterns. In nature's pecking order, humans fall under predators, while our hoofed friends belong in the prey category. This predator-prey dynamic plays out when we ride them—with us being on top (literally), exerting control over an animal that was naturally designed for freedom and to fear the potentially deadly predator on its back.

Think about this for a second. Horses, originally born wild animals, are all strapped in with another animal's hide in the form of a girth and saddle snugged up nice and tight. Add to that little combo a predator plopped right on top. The human predator with ambiguous "asks," and the usual bit of fear and apprehension involved with riding, is enough to terrify most horses.

Consider a scenario where your toddler hides behind you at the sight of a stranger—pretty standard toddler behavior rooted in fear of unknown entities—a trait shared by our equine companions, too. Horses have an innate survival instinct that makes them wary of potential threats—an evolutionary hangover from their days in the wild when predators hunted them. It doesn't usually work out so well for the rider when your horse tries to hide behind a jump standard because someone moved the muck bucket over to the left a tiny two inches.

Just ask my own horse, Milo.

He would tell you that a scary mounting block in a suspicious place; it was enough for him to take off at a gallop for three laps and a cross-rail jump or two—all while I had simply asked for the trot! Unexpected and continuous speed is not something I chase after these days. I did end up in the dirt that day with a bleeding lip... I was thrilled with that outcome, over the possible hip fracture or misplaced dentures. (The dentures part is a joke for now; however, that may need to be edited by the time I finish this little book.)

Similar to how you reassure your scared toddler by holding his hand tightly and whispering comforting words into his ear, your horse needs reassurance from you—the rider—to help calm him down during stressful situations. Ambiguous cues (or "asks" in equestrian terms) are frightening for a horse. He has handed safety and control over to his rider. The rider is now the eyes of both the horse and the rider, especially regarding the horse's blind spots. This is super important to understanding riding, and so more on that later.

Recognize similarities between managing toddlers and horses. Understand that their fears stem from instincts and can be mitigated with reassurance. This, in itself, is an effective confidence booster.

When dealing with a particularly anxious or frightened horse—something like a toddler throwing an extreme tantrum—you may need to employ advanced measures. Consider bringing in a professional trainer who can employ specialized techniques to calm the animal down. As far as your actual toddler goes, consider bringing in grandma, or someone who doesn't take any guff from "kids these days!"

Bad advice often circulated in riding communities is to "show the horse who's boss" by asserting dominance. This approach is counterproductive, similar to shouting at a scared child—it only heightens their fear and leaves a lasting impression.

Horses, like toddlers, need gentle handling, reassurance, consistency, and they need to feel safe. In any event, a reputable lesson barn will do its absolute best to match the rider with the temperament and skill level of the horse. Another huge help when learning to ride is for the lesson barn to allocate the same horse to you for many consecutive weeks. Keeping the horse and its quirks and levels of responsiveness the same for a new rider takes away a lot of the initial newness and changing or moving parts. I tell new parents that every time you put any rider together with a horse, it's a "gong show." Both will be moody. Both are usually hungry during lessons. The horse might be older and grumpy. The rider is often tired, scared, wiggly, or a combination.

Understanding why horses react as they do will give you "aha" moments of realization. You'll begin seeing parallels between managing your two-year-old and your horse. If you are lucky enough to be past the toddler phase at home and you think you're out of the woods, look out; there are plenty of adults with toddler-like behavior. You'll see parallels with them, too.

This book does wonders for mental health. Hopefully, you will find the fun in situations that used to cause discomfort. Horses have a wonderful way of shifting our perspectives. I mean paradigm-sized shifts. Humor and horses provide a fabulous lift away from reality—even if only while you have your nose in this book.

———

Points to Ponder:

• Horses are like toddlers: What you see is what you get.

• As prey animals ridden by predators (humans), horses may exhibit fear or stress. They hand over control to their rider. Sitting quietly and confidently on a horse is essential to good riding.

• To mitigate these reactions, offer reassurance just as you would comfort a scared toddler.

• In extreme situations where the horse seems overly anxious or frightened, consider hiring a professional trainer for help.

• Avoid harsh methods of asserting dominance; instead, opt for gentle handling.

Pro Tip:

Every interaction with your horse should be based on understanding and empathy—not domination and fear. Just like raising children requires patience and love, training horses demands similar qualities plus a mountain of consistency and clarity.

Movements on and around horses should always be "tai chi" slow.

CHAPTER 7

THE EQUINE TODDLER TANGO

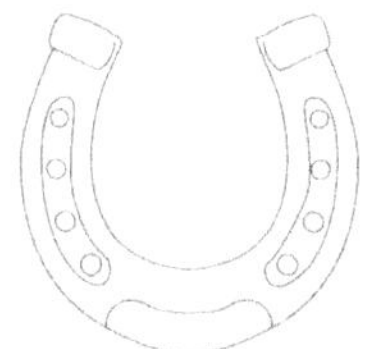

In the grand circus of life, where the ringmaster juggles responsibilities and the audience watches with rapt attention, two of the most entertaining acts share the spotlight: horses and human toddlers. At first glance, they may have seemed worlds apart, but upon closer inspection, one might find they have more in common than one would think.

The Art of Communication

Let's start with their unique communication styles. Horses are the poets of the animal kingdom, expressing themselves through whinnies, neighs, and the occasional stomp of a hoof. They have a rich vocabulary that ranges from the soft nicker of satisfaction to the loud whinny of "I'm hungry!" Similarly, toddlers have their own expressive repertoire, consisting of squeals, cries, and the occasionally well-placed tantrum. If a horse could speak English, I imagine it would say something like, "Excuse me, I'm ready for my snack," while a toddler might just throw their entire snack on the floor and wail, "I wanted the blue one!"

Both species excel in non-verbal communication too. Horses communicate with their ears, tails, and body posture. A pinned ear can mean, "Back off, buddy," while a swishing tail might indicate, "I'm just gonna stand here and look majestic." On the other hand, toddlers master the art of the pout, the glare, and the dramatic flop to the floor when they don't get their way. It's a universal language known only to those who have survived the toddler years–or a close encounter with a horse.

The Snack Attack

Next, let's talk about food. Horses are notorious for their grazing habits, munching on hay and grass as if they're at an all-you-can-eat-all-day-long buffet. They nibble leisurely, savoring each bite like a fine dining experience. Meanwhile, toddlers approach snack time with the intensity of a hungry horse at a feed trough. There's no grazing here; it's all about the rapid-fire consumption and the inevitable aftermath of crumbs scattered like confetti across the living room floor.

But here's the kicker: both horses and toddlers can be incredibly picky. A horse might turn its nose up at a perfectly good apple if it's not sliced just right, while a toddler may reject broccoli as if it were poison, despite having devoured it yesterday. It's a delicate dance of feeding that requires patience and a willingness to cater to whims. Sigh.

The Need for Space

Now, let's dive into their need for personal space. Horses are majestic creatures that often prefer their own company, especially when they're feeling particularly regal. They'll stand alone in their paddock, surveying their domain like a king on a throne. On the other hand, toddlers have a different take on personal space: they have absolutely no concept. They'll cling to your leg while you're trying to make a phone call and, somehow, they always find a way to invade your bubble when you least expect it.

However, both can exhibit extreme independence when it suits them. A horse might decide to wander off for a snack break during a ride, while a toddler will suddenly declare, "I can do it myself!" as they attempt to dress themselves in a tangle of clothing with the end result being a cross between Boy George and a colorblind clown.

The Energy Levels

Energy levels? Let's just say horses and toddlers are similar to rockets fueled by sugar and hay. Horses can gallop around a field with an exuberance that leaves onlookers in awe, while toddlers have an endless reservoir of energy that allows them to bounce off walls—literally.

But just like that, both can flip the switch and enter a state of complete relaxation. A horse can go from a full gallop to napping in the sun in mere seconds, while a toddler can transition from a whirlwind of activity to a gentle snore, often in the middle of a playdate. I wish I still had the nerve to simply drop off to sleep when my body needed me to. It's as if they've mastered the art of sudden shutdowns, leaving parents —and horse owners—wondering what just happened.

The Affection Factor

Finally, let's touch on affection. Horses are surprisingly loving creatures, forming strong bonds with their humans. They'll nuzzle and nicker, expressing their love in subtle yet meaningful ways. Toddlers, on the other hand, have a more direct approach. They'll shower you with sticky hugs and spontaneous kisses, often followed by a request for a snack or a drink.

In conclusion, while horses and human toddlers may seem like an odd pairing, they share a delightful array of similarities and differences. Both of these irresistible forms of life share endearing and exasperating tendencies. They teach us patience, resilience, and the importance of snacks–because if there's one thing we can all agree on, life is better with a bit of hay and a lot of love. So, the next time you find yourself at a stable or a playroom, remember: whether it's a horse or a toddler, you're in for an unpredictable adventure filled with laughter, love, and perhaps a few well-timed messes. Though, horse disasters are quite a lot more costly than the mishaps caused by the toddlers of this world.

Communication styles of horses and toddlers exhibit both similarities and distinct differences. Here are the key differences:

Horses:

1. Vocalizations: Horses use a range of sounds to communicate, including whinnies, nickers, and snorts. Each sound conveys different emotions or messages, such as excitement, comfort, or distress.

2. Body Language: Horses rely heavily on body language. They communicate through posture, ear position, tail movement, and facial expressions. For example, pinned ears may indicate irritation, while licking and chewing suggest relaxation and comfort.

3. Nonverbal Cues: Horses are attuned to subtle cues in their environment and the behavior of other horses or handlers. They may respond to the slightest change in body language from their human or fellow

horses. They will also pick up on moods and whether a person is congruent or not... does the big smile on the human's face match the person's insides? A horse will not engage with anyone who is incongruent if it is left up to the horse.

4. Social Signals: In a herd, horses use social behaviors like grooming, nuzzling, or standing close to one another to express affection and establish bonds within their group. Toddlers may be doing that sort of thing one minute, and then clobber you over the noggin the next.

Bonking people on the noggin is the mere tip of the iceberg of a toddler's potentially giant and comprehensive disaster plan.

Toddlers:

1. Vocalizations: Toddlers primarily use verbal sounds, ranging from babbling to words and phrases. Their vocal expressions vary widely depending on their mood—happy squeals for joy or cries, grunts, and screams for frustration.

2. Gestures: Toddlers use hand gestures, pointing, and facial expressions to communicate their needs and feelings. They may wave, shake their heads, or use exaggerated facial expressions to convey excitement or displeasure.

3. Tantrums: Unlike horses, toddlers may resort to tantrums as a form of communication when they are overwhelmed, frustrated, or unable to express themselves verbally. This can often be a dramatic display that captures much unwanted attention.

4. Imitation: Toddlers learn communication through imitation, mimicking sounds and words from adults or peers. This learning process is integral to their development and understanding of language. This learning process of theirs also drops you in the sh*t when they decide to share your private and top-secret F-bombs with your in-laws, and they already pretend you don't exist. (Based on a true story.)

While both horses and toddlers rely on vocalizations and body language to communicate, horses emphasize nonverbal cues and body posture, while toddlers engage more in vocal expression and gestures. Horses have a more instinctual form of communication based on their social structures, while toddlers learn and develop their language skills and emotional expressions through imitation and interaction.

Understanding how horses are like big toddlers can help us anticipate horse behavior and understand what might otherwise seem confusing and scary. Remember this as we discuss other aspects of horses in depth–when something seems foreign or surprising, just remind yourself: "Horses are just 1200-pound toddlers."

CHAPTER 8

SPEAKING OF PECKING ORDER: THE HIDDEN HIERARCHY AMONG HORSES

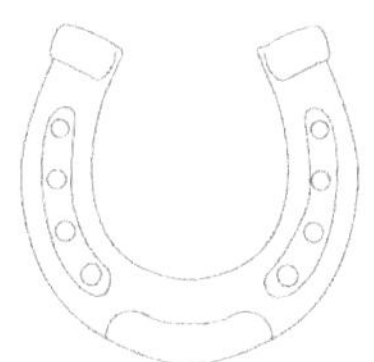

Just like in any other group of social animals, horses establish their own hierarchies—a phenomenon often referred to as the "pecking order." This invisible structure is paramount for maintaining peace and stability within the herd. However, it also presents unique challenges and considerations for us as caretakers and riders.

Horses are naturally gregarious creatures with complex social structures dating back thousands of years. They lived in herds long before they were domesticated by humans, relying on this hierarchy system for survival. Each member had a specific role and position determined by various factors such as age, gender, temperament, size, or strength.

Up until February 26th, 2024, the head of our herd was Razor. Razor had some issues. He was ancient, grumpy, humble and kind. He was also a fellow Canadian. Despite all those less-than-perfect qualities, he had the herd's respect and was the boss. He would always come in first. He would go out first. He could do anything he decided he wanted to do, first.

So, how can you identify these roles? Often, it's through observing subtle cues in behavior or body language. The dominant horse may assert control over resources like food or water troughs/tubs while others wait their turn—one clear indication of hierarchy levels. Much like great Aunt Rosary, who always got to be number one at the Thanksgiving buffet! She was precious and she went first.

Let me give you an actual horse example: Doc is one of our more dominant horses. Actually, he is a naughty frat boy. He is the poke and run kind of horse. If Doc needs to be kept in for a later lesson, he has to be moved inside a different barn. He has to be able to see another horse, or he paces and stomps and sweats and almost turns himself inside-out.

We have a herd of horses here at Salko Farm. Here is the list of the first 10, in order of dominance:

Jett

Doc

Zipper

Milo

Prince (These top five "turn in" in this exact order, or else!)

Charlie

Oakley

Aquillo

Triscut

Paul

We also watch out for interactions. Teddy is always last. He's very confused a lot of the time. Plus, a total introvert. As of November 2025, Harley is back at Salko Farm. He's having a hard time settling here. He is a low man on the pole and stays back to feel safe.

In my experience working with these magnificent beasts, I've seen how disrupting this natural pecking order can lead to stress and conflict within the herd. Say you decide to introduce a new horse into your existing group without proper introduction protocols—this could result in chaos because each animal would try to assert its dominance.

Pro Tip:

Understanding horses' hierarchical structure is essential for their well-being and effective management and handling.

Consider an example from my time at a ranch when we introduced a young gelding (Paul) into our established herd. Initially, Paul was greeted with hostility. The first night that we turned him out, the other geldings knocked him down repeatedly until he needed to be rescued from the herd. The neighbor who overlooks our pasture called to let us know that there was a horse down. They'd kicked Paul in the head, and he was down.

It sometimes takes months to introduce and integrate a new horse into an existing, long-established herd. We've integrated over 300 horses here at Salko Farm.

The power dynamics within a horse herd are fascinatingly complex but also very natural. When you step into their world, you are essentially stepping into an animal kingdom with its own rules and regulations. Lord help you if you should step in between a dominant horse and a bottom-of-the-barrel horse on the way to the feed bin. The dominant horse does not care who is in his way; he will knock anything or anyone down to be the first to the food! It is obnoxious and takes some getting used to.

Let's reflect on a case study showing how impactful understanding these dynamics can be. Dr. Katherine Houpt of Cornell University researched feral horse bands in Wyoming and found that mares usually lead family groups while stallions protect against threats.

Not all conflicts within a horse herd are negative—sometimes, they're necessary for establishing or reestablishing order. Some conflicts occur when a younger bully needs an intervention; he won't stop pestering an older, less-spirited horse in the herd. It happens. The bully will usually find himself being marched away by a group of elders who have decided the underdog horses need some peace.

———

Points to Ponder:

• Horses have evolved to live in well-defined social structures.

• The pecking order reduces conflict by establishing clear roles.

• Human intervention can disrupt this balance if not done thoughtfully.

It is important to introduce new horses slowly to allow them time to understand their position within the hierarchy without causing undue stress or conflict. A herd of horses has been known to collectively bully a new, weaker horse. It is one of the qualities sometimes found in horses that is very upsetting to me.

A notable statistic is from the Equine Science (4th Edition) by Rick Parker, B.S., M.S., Ph.D. Typically, one horse emerges as the leader or "alpha" in every group of five horses, regardless of breed or location.

To navigate this complex equine world successfully, here are some action steps:

• Observe herds whenever you are able–watch their interactions closely.

• Introduce new members gradually–use separate paddocks initially, then supervised mingling sessions.

• Respect their space–don't force interactions or changes.

• Provide adequate resources–ensure each horse has access to food, water, and shelter without having to fight for it.

• Seek professional advice if needed–particularly when dealing with aggressive or anxious horses.

P.S. Please note that all of the above action steps would also apply to your beloved teenagers. Cue to laugh.

Note: Younger horses overall—five years old or less–can do massive amounts of damage to an elderly herd. The young ones do not know when to quit the games and have *way* more energy than the older horses. They also have way less common sense!

As you explore the world of horses further, understanding their social structure becomes indispensable. Knowledge is power and confidence where horses are concerned. It allows you to manage your herd effectively, reduces conflicts and stress among them, and leads to a more harmonious coexistence. So, remember, patience is key in managing these magnificent creatures. Take time to understand their world; after all, we're visitors to their kingdom. Again, teenagers.

CHAPTER 9

HORSES AS TEACHERS

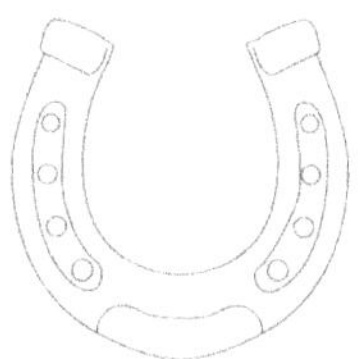

As you watch your child's fascination with these wonderful creatures, you may wonder about the connection between horses and humans. After all, they're just animals, right? In my years of experience working with these majestic creatures, I've found that horses can be profound teachers and healers.

Horses have roamed our planet for over 50 million years. They've been companions to humans for millennia, playing crucial roles in transportation, agriculture, and warfare. But their significance extends beyond mere utility; horses possess an innate ability to mirror human emotions and intentions–an attribute that has endeared them to us throughout history. The simple truth is this, humans have still only merely scratched the surface of our true understanding of horses and how they positively affect us. We truly have no idea.

Fun Fact: A horse will mirror and match a human's biorhythms.

Our relationship with horses is deeply rooted in a shared emotional and energetic landscape. Horses are highly sensitive creatures capable of perceiving the slightest shifts in human emotion or intention. This sensitivity stems from their nature as prey animals; they evolved to detect subtle environmental changes to survive. They operate on a vibrational level that far surpasses that of humans.

You've heard it said that we are all made of energy and that higher vibrations are associated with more positivity, happiness, and even productivity. Higher vibration implies less chaos of the mind. Now, let's get to the main point–how exactly do these equine qualities teach us about ourselves?

Firstly, horses act as mirrors, reflecting our inner state back at us. Their keen sense of perception picks up on our feelings even before we consciously recognize them–a trait that has earned them the nickname "lie detectors." If you're anxious but trying to mask it under a facade of calmness, a horse will see right through it. A horse will almost roll his eyes at a human who is out of congruence. Your big smile doesn't match your upset tummy or chaotic brain... a horse will call bullsh*t. Horses cannot relate to a human with a chaotic brain. A chaotic brain (yep, three times in a row) is like fingernails on a chalkboard to a horse... it is the exact same for humans. Guess what? They call it anxiety and then ruin their own physical health and all the health and most of the happiness of their closest friends and family members. **The subconscious mind will help you avoid it all rather than allow you to slow down to begin to unravel some of the parts of your life that you may have had to shove down your throat for a time, due to your age and level of authority, and maybe not being able to "speak back" at that time.**

The truth is that the human race right now is floundering. Media has such a strong grip and constant impact on our feelings of comparison, scarcity, and separation that we subconsciously want more and more outside material possessions. Horses know that happiness comes from a peaceful and present state of being. If humans actually knew they have the power to stop to analyze and then ditch any negative looping ruminating or pondering that is causing the dis-ease in your tummy or head, wouldn't they all be doing it? We hope that with our next book–W.A.I.T. - What Am I Thinking–we will be able to simply lay out for the general public, exactly how to slow down enough to start to sift and discard the stale and outdated ingredients from your past.

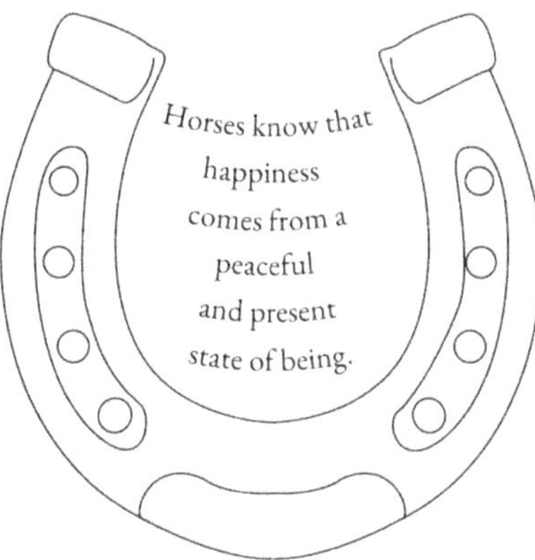

A horse's ability to perceive our true feelings encourages authenticity and congruence within ourselves.

Their perceptiveness also extends to detecting incongruences between our actions and intentions. A horse responds positively when your actions align with your intent (congruence) and resists when there's discordance. This interaction teaches us the importance of aligning our thoughts, words, and deeds—an essential lesson in integrity. A horse is not interested in even being next to a person with fast thoughts in their mind. Horses interact with humans only when the humans are authentically right here, right now, not off somewhere else in their heads with no present awareness. That second scenario often ends in a human foot losing to a horse hoof when vying for the same ground space.

In my experience, chaos in the mind comes from not knowing our core values. How can we make effective decisions if we don't know our raison d'être? Whoa, that was a slight dip into a topic for another day.

In analyzing the horse-human connection, it's fascinating to note that horses have energy centers or chakras similar to ours. These chakras are vortexes of energy within the body related to our physical, emotional, and spiritual health. Horses have the same seven primary chakras humans do: root, sacral, solar plexus, heart, throat, third eye, and crown. They also have an extra chakra called the Brachial Key. I highly recommend the book *Riding with the Chakras* by Christina Stinchcomb for more on this topic. Christina's book does a fabulous job of explaining exactly how these affect both ourselves and the horses.

Case Study: In a 2005 study published in "Society & Animals," researchers found evidence supporting the therapeutic benefits of equine-assisted therapies. Participants reported reductions in anxiety and depression levels after engaging with horses. Touched by a Horse has pages of scientific research to back this up at www.touchedbyahorse.com.

Horses can play a pivotal role in enhancing human mental health. This is bigger than people understand. Horses help humans excavate and release major blockages: often blockages previously well outside their consciousness. The horse-human bond isn't just anecdotal; LOTS of science backs up this unique relationship. More and more research is showing that interacting with horses can lower blood pressure and heart rate, reduce stress, and reduce symptoms of anxiety and depression. Horses have also been aiding veterans through their post-war ailments for several decades. The results are amazingly positive. Check out Nancy De Santis in New Mexico. Horses for Heroes Cowboy Up! is a ranch set up specifically for people experiencing PTSD, which Nancy calls Post-Traumatic Spiritual Dissonance (www.horsesforheroes.org).

Here are some incredible facts about horses:

- The average horse's heart weighs approximately 10 pounds.
- A horse's eyes are among the largest of any land mammal.
- Horses use their ears, eyes, and nostrils to express their mood.
- Horses express their feelings through nonverbal cues, an important reminder for humans about communication beyond words.

Somatics are such an important part of all aspects of life. The more we slow down, the more aware we become of ourselves and somatics in general. I've slowed down so much that I am aware of bird sounds that I had never heard before. Colors are brighter and I am always feeling like there is enough time for everything now. This is all due to my head being about 15% as busy as it used to be, all day, every day.

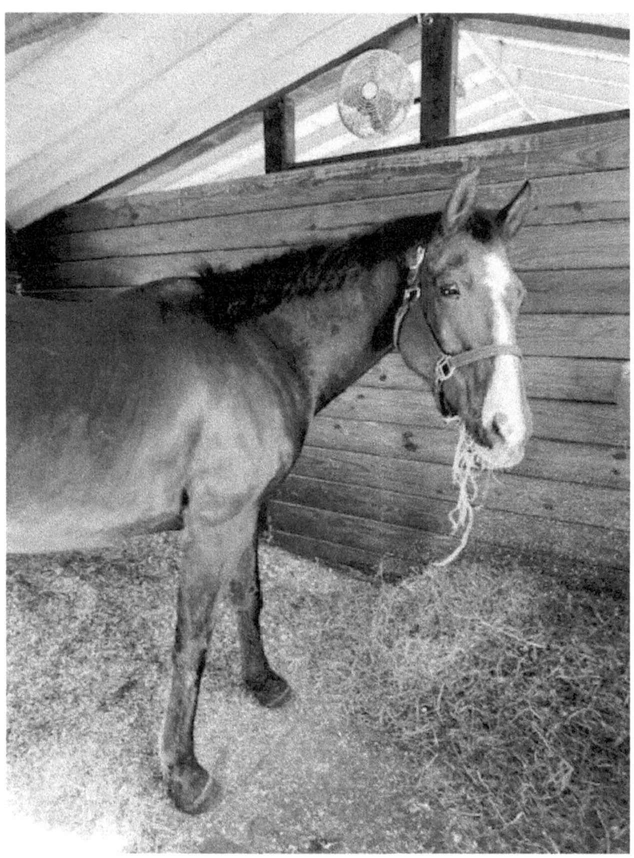

We need to actively look for ways to interact with horses to be able to fully appreciate the wisdom these creatures provide us. Here's how you might begin:

1. Spend time observing a horse without any agenda—watch it move around its environment.

2. Pay attention to your emotions around a horse—are you calm? Restless? Anxious? Are you suddenly feeling weepy?

3. Practice mindfulness while grooming them or cleaning their stalls—these tasks aren't chores but opportunities for connection. Opportunities to stand right here, right now, and experience the closeness of these magical creations.

4. Take riding lessons to build a deeper bond, not with competition as an objective. Grooming and tacking for your own lesson is strongly suggested as a time to really bond with the horse that is about to provide you with a ride.

5. Consider Equine Gestalt™ therapy or coaching as an avenue for self-discovery. Or even as a second career option!

Engaging with horses in mindful, intentional ways offers us profound insights into ourselves and our emotions.

Though they may be large and strong, horses are sensitive beings with much to teach us about authenticity, connection, and living in the moment. Their wisdom is unique–a blend of ancient instinct and evolved understanding–with a handful of good ole toddler. So, next time you encounter these magnificent creatures, take a moment to appreciate their unbridled wisdom–they truly are energetic healers in their own right.

CHAPTER 10

Polyvagal Theory: The Impact on Humans and What It Means in Real Life

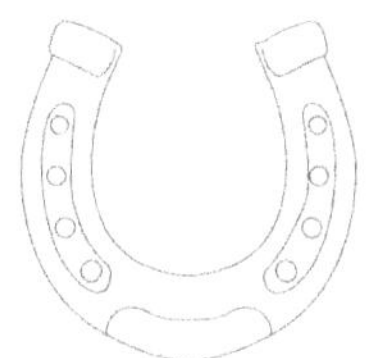

Horses can have a profound impact on people's nervous systems, especially in the context of the Polyvagal Theory, which focuses on how the vagus nerve influences emotional regulation, social connection, and fear responses. Horses can positively influence people's nervous systems by promoting relaxation, emotional awareness, and connection.

Horses are known for their ability to create a sense of calm and safety. Their large, non-threatening presence can help individuals activate their parasympathetic nervous system, which is associated with relaxation and social engagement. Being around horses can help lower anxiety and stress levels.

Horses are highly attuned to human emotions and body language. This non-verbal interaction can help individuals become more aware of their own emotional states and reactions. This heightened awareness can facilitate emotional regulation and improve connections with others.

The concept of mirror neurons suggests that horses can reflect the emotional states of people. If a person is anxious, a horse may become anxious as well, which can help the person recognize and address their own feelings.

As I have mentioned many times in this book, horses are like toddlers. Toddlers are "selfish" in that they know no better than to be out for number one. When an adult human is lost in their own head, in a typical-for-today "sympathetic state" of their nervous system, that head noise causes discomfort within the horse. Based on energy and science, the horse hears this as an uncomfortable static and automatically works to clear that noise. They want people to be present, which means being fully present in their bodies and out of their spinning minds. How much of what is on our minds most of the day is simply noise and repetitive loops of nonsense? Most of it.

Horses energetically balance *any* human within their range (20 - 30 feet) as a selfish way to clear the noisy static and restore peace of mind for themselves, and then ultimately, the unsuspecting human. This is really, really big news. It's not *new* news, but it's a different way of understanding the extremely special emotional and physical connection between horses and humans.

The nervous system state that horses naturally and organically lift us into is called the ventral vagal state. The ventral vagal state, as explained by Stephen W. Porges as part of the Polyvagal Theory, is a state where safety is felt within the body to a level that allows guards to come down, perspectives to shift, and wider-mindedness to be experienced.

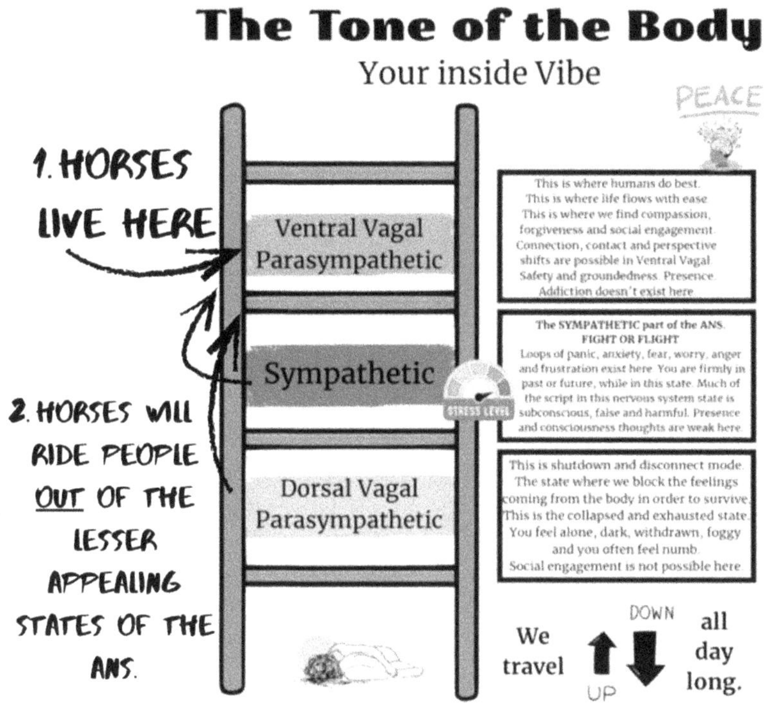

This allows us to feel and express gratitude, compassion, self-compassion, forgiveness, joy, and overall "generosity of spirit," towards self and others.

The shift into the ventral vagal state is somewhat impacted by the energy centers (Chakras) and mainly by the innate ability of the horse to co-regulate with humans. The horse is ten times bigger than the human and has a much better sense of being present and therefore almost always hangs out in the safe and social ventral vagal state. Since the horse is right here, right now, in their bodies, they possess the strength and resilience to draw us into their calm and safe space. The static that horses hear from the human brain hits them like a ton of bricks, and they will selfishly work to regulate the human out of their busy brains and into their hearts. Horses are conscious and present by nature. Humans are not. It's safe to say that humans are only in conscious contact with what they are feeling in their bodies for a small fraction of any waking day.

What does this mean in real life? It means that one of the best ways to get your nervous system back in balance and in a state of comfort and safety (ventral vagal) is to stand next to a horse. Humans cannot think their way back into a state of calm (ventral vagal). Their bodies have to take them there. One way a person can achieve this is by taking control of their breath. Slowing your breathing rate tells the body to slow down, in its own language. Box breathing is another great body tool.

The work we are sharing with Recovery Rehab Centers across America is yielding impressive research, demonstrating solid and consistent improvement in how residents feel regarding connection, hopefulness, coping skills, and peace of mind after spending time with a horse.

For more information on this subject, please email us at janesalko66@gmail.com.

BOX BREATHING

16 Count Breathing
(for immediate
Parasympathetic benefit)

2 ~ Hold for FOUR

through
the
nose.

1 Breathe
in for
FOUR

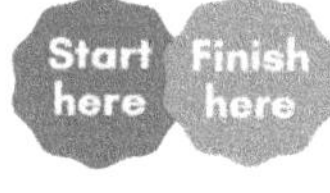

3 Breathe
out for
FOUR

with an
open-mouthed
smile with
a sigh.

4 ~ Hold for FOUR

Start at the bottom left of the square.
Take a deep breath in through your nose for four counts.
Hold your breath for four counts (or pause there for four counts)
Breathe out with a sigh through your open-mouthed smile for full somatic advantage.
Like the OM sound, attaching any sound will automatically connect mind and body through vibration.

CHAPTER 11

THE UNDERLYING HUMAN HEALING ASPECT OF HORSES

ALMOST TOO MANY TO MENTION!

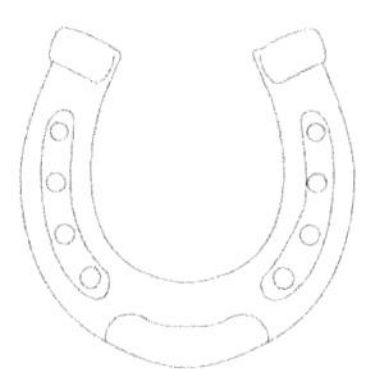

Exposing your horse-obsessed child (or self) to horses may seem simple and important only inasmuch as how it lights up your child. However, there's a reason equine-assisted therapy exists: horses seem to hold a magical power for healing and calming. For centuries, these energetically in-tuned creatures have not only served as physical laborers and companions but also played a significant role in our spiritual and emotional well-being.

Horses are innately empathetic animals, capable of sensing humans' emotions and responding accordingly. This sensitivity stems from their history as prey animals, where survival depended on their ability to interpret subtle shifts in herd dynamics or potential predator behaviors. Over time, these abilities have evolved into an extraordinary capacity for emotional connection in the form of assessing intention. Again, vibrational and energy related.

A hungry mountain lion walks across a ridge, approximately one hundred feet from a wild herd of horses. The head of the herd, whether a lead mare or stallion, sends a vibration through the herd, and they run away from the predator. You thought I was kidding about the vibration.

As an aside, the more open you can get your own mind, the easier your life will be.

The same mountain lion eats a deer for lunch and later walks right back across the same ridge. The horses slowly grazed their way back to the original lush pasture they had fled earlier when the big old lion passed them again. The horses remain as they are, casually grazing. As the mountain lion is no longer hungry, the horses know they do not need to flee. No danger is presented to their herd in the form of a belly-stuffed-full-of-deer mountain lion. Seems like another hard-to-believe fairy tale?

Here's more. Interestingly enough, horses can mirror back our feelings. They will mirror both those we think openly and those we try to suppress. They respond most positively when they sense authenticity within us–a state achieved when we are fully present in our bodies rather than lost in our thoughts.

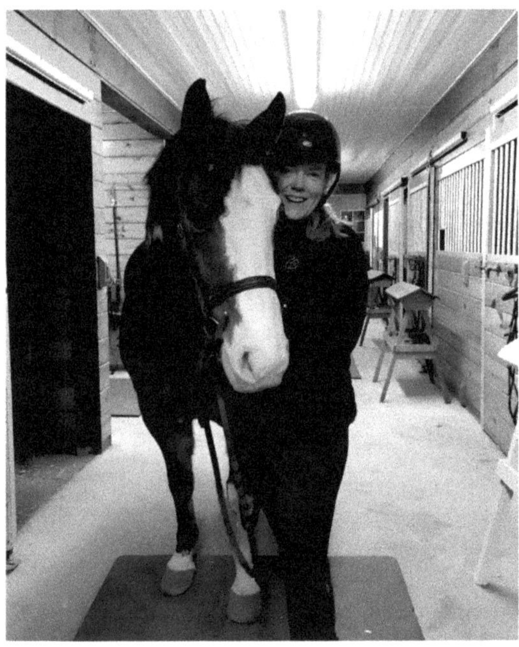

Horses help us find ourselves by making us more aware of our body language and nonverbal cues–important factors often overshadowed by verbal communication's dominance and the fact that most people are spinning too fast to see much of anything. When interacting with a horse, your slightest movements can convey strong messages that the horse reacts to accordingly. This heightened awareness makes you more conscious of yourself in the present moment. You will likely slow down and check in with your body, maybe long enough to avoid an unnecessary conflict. For your toes' sake, I hope presence keeps them from under the 1,200-pound toddler's big hooves.

Being around horses cultivates overall mindfulness—an essential step toward finding your true self.

The evidence supporting this theory is plentiful; I can't say it enough–many studies have documented the therapeutic effects of equine-assisted therapies and any human-equine interaction.

One such study published in 2018 by BMC Psychiatry found that Equine-Assisted Psychotherapy (EAP) significantly improved mental health outcomes among participants who have various psychological disorders such as PTSD and depression. This improved not only the PTSD of veterans but also any form of traumatic experiences.

"Until you have loved an animal, a part of your soul stays unawakened."
–Anatole France

I firmly believe in this quote. Letting your guard down when animals are close by involves vulnerability. It may be a chance to drop your tough exterior and allow *your* voice to escape from your mouth.

Consider Anna Blake's story–an internationally recognized dressage clinician who suffered from chronic anxiety until she uncovered the healing power of horses. Blake recounts how each interaction with horses taught her to be more present and aware, ultimately helping her overcome anxiety and return to living a happy and fulfilled life.

Anna's story brings us to another crucial aspect of equine-assisted therapy–it helps align our chakras/energy centers. Maintaining balanced chakras is believed to promote physical and emotional well-being in various spiritual practices. The quiet presence of a horse can help ground you in your body, aiding in balancing the root chakra–the foundation for building inner peace and confidence. There is so much to be learned about chakras and how our blockages can be cleared with the help of horses. A horse will turn 180 degrees and place its big hind end about one foot from the human–sending solid root chakra energy to the human standing there perhaps feeling unstable and not so grounded.

A study published by Explore Journal in 2018 revealed that interacting with horses increased positive emotions and reduced participants' stress levels, indicating hugely potential benefits for chakra alignment.

> *"Interacting with horses can help with balancing our energy centers/chakras."*

Horses are also instrumental in facilitating human connections. When we're fully present, free from distractions, we're better able to connect not only with ourselves but also others around us.

I've noted some fascinating facts in my years of experience dealing with equine-assisted services.

———

Fun Facts:

• Horses have over 17 different facial expressions. Some will argue there are many more.

• They communicate using subtle body language cues.

• Their heart rate lowers when around humans who are calm and grounded. They match biorhythms. A kind horse will detect an anxious human with an elevated heart rate and work hard to slow the human's heart rate down. A younger or less experienced horse (with less professional training) may feel that rider's anxiety and try to run away from it. A terrified, ambiguous, unconfident rider is about all a horse can take. Chaotic mind with nervous vibes - that's enough to make a horse simply take off to get away from it all. It feels really unsafe and will often run.

Good luck to the rider unless they are good at shapeshifting into a professional jockey while on the fly?

Horses' highly intuitive nature makes them excellent facilitators for fostering self-awareness and personal growth. They are especially brilliant at showing up as a partner in coaching. Check out Hippie Cowgirl Retreats for more information about horses, personal development, growth, and dusty good times for women in the Arizona desert 🌵!

Finally, here's your action plan:

1. Spend time around horses without an agenda—just observe their behavior.

2. Practice mindfulness during these interactions—stay attuned to your feelings and thoughts.

3. Notice how the horse reacts to your presence—are they drawn toward you, or do they maintain distance? Horses, like humans, are both introverts and extroverts. Truth!

4. Reflect on these experiences, journaling about them if possible.

5. Try incorporating a few Equine Gestalt™ sessions into your wellness routine. The science behind Equine Gestalt™ healing and improved overall mood and life outlook is available on the Touched by a Horse website: www.touchedbyahorse.com.

This is important enough to repeat—**horses offer us an authentic connection that stimulates self-discovery and personal growth.** Their intuitive nature and heightened sensitivity to our emotions make them excellent companions on our journey toward inner peace and well-being. I have seen this work, and it's incredibly positive and hugely beneficial. Many of my closest friends have seen a lifetime of growth in just two years spent in the Equine Gestaltist™ certification program. This often includes the complete removal of outdated, self-limiting information. Sometimes referred to as a Troll-ectomy...

In the next chapter, we'll cover how this unique connection between humans and horses shows up specifically in work with children. This is largely to do with the fact that children are more horse-like than adults.

They are more like the bright light of joy we are all born with, before we cover it all up with the introjections of others and the garbage we tell ourselves about ourselves. All negative. Well, mostly.

Equine Assisted Services—what are they really?

The bond between humans and horses is a tale as old as time. From ancient civilizations to modern-day equestrian sports, these majestic creatures have captivated our hearts and minds for centuries. Yet their role extends beyond companionship or transportation; horses can play a pivotal role in mental health, particularly for children.

Over the years, I've seen firsthand how powerful this interaction can be. The unique dynamic between horses and humans transcends age barriers, creating an environment that nurtures growth, understanding, and empathy. This chapter considers why such connections exist and provides actionable strategies to maximize these benefits.

Interactions with horses can foster emotional well-being in children because they require compassion and understanding that are not always present in their typical social circles. Horses respond to kindness, patience, and consistency—values we wish to instill in youngsters early on. At least, that was what it was like when I was a wee one.

Interactions with horses promote compassion, patience, and consistency among children.

Scientific studies corroborate these observations. For instance, research published by the American Psychological Association (APA) found that therapeutic riding programs significantly improved confidence levels among youths aged 10-14 after just five sessions. These boosts in confidence levels are even more apparent with Equine Gestalt sessions.

Consider Gertie's story—an introverted 8-year-old struggling with self-esteem issues due to bullying at school. Her therapist suggested equine-assisted services as a supplemental treatment strategy alongside traditional counseling methods. Gertie was initially apprehensive but soon formed an incredible bond with Tinkerbell, a gentle mare who mirrored her own shy demeanor.

Gertie's transformation is an ideal example of this connection's potency–she began expressing herself freely around Tinkerbell, which gradually translated into her daily life. She was no longer the quiet girl in the corner but actively participated in class discussions and group activities. This happens more times than not, and I'm not kidding.

I can't tell you how many times a young girl has begun coming to our farm for weekly lessons. She starts out shy and very quiet–barely saying boo to a goose. They look at adults through their bangs (fringe if you are in the UK) and answer in very low tones, almost inaudible. Within a few weeks to a month, almost every shy girl (and boy) finds some confidence within themselves and marches onto the property with their heads held high and their shoulders thrown back. They smile and wave hello FIRST! To me, this is a magical part of horse farm life.

Equine Gestalt™, in particular, can profoundly impact self-esteem and confidence levels in people of any age.

Points to Ponder:

• Horses have an innate ability to mirror human emotions, helping people recognize their feelings more accurately.

• Regular interaction with horses can significantly reduce stress levels– I've already referenced much scientific proof.

• It encourages physical activity–a crucial component of mental wellness.

• It inevitably allows for a more authentic connection with self, for many. Awareness is so valuable, abundantly available, and likely to be found in this work.

Interaction with horses offers a holistic approach to mental wellness– incorporating emotional understanding and awareness, physical activity, and stress reduction.

In any given year, according to the National Institutes of Health, about 20% of children experience mental health issues. With resources stretched thin and conventional treatments not consistently effective, alternative methods such as Equine Assisted Services (EAS) show promise.

Now that you understand why this bond is so useful, let's explore how you can foster it effectively:

1. **Start Small:** Begin with gentle interactions such as feeding or petting before moving on to riding sessions.

2. **Be Consistent:** Consistency is key in building trust–schedule regular visits for maximum benefits.

3. **Keep Expectations Realistic:** Remember that progress may be slow initially–it's important not to rush the process. Horses love things to be "tai chi" slow.

4. **Involve Professionals:** Ensure safety by involving professionals trained in EAS during the initial stages.

5. **Celebrate Progress:** Acknowledge every success, no matter how small–it boosts confidence and motivates continued efforts.

Embrace these strategies diligently–the rewards will undoubtedly outweigh any initial hesitations or challenges encountered along the way!

Warning:

Be aware of many completely online "Equine Therapy" courses offered. Many of them are not the real deal. Usually, the longer an educator's history, the better.

CHAPTER 12

VETERANS AND THE POWER OF HORSES

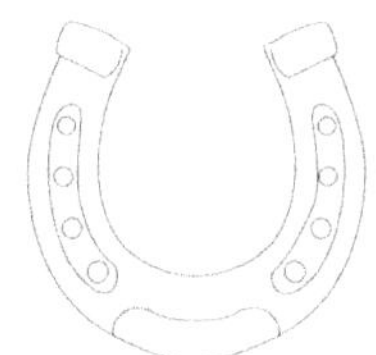

While much of the focus is on horse-loving children, nearly everything said here is relevant to any human interacting with horses. However, there's another special group of people where equine benefits are worth highlighting.

Veterans are a specific population that experiences some of the most transforming times with horses. There are many studies demonstrating the significant positive impact that horses can have on the mental health and overall well-being of veterans, particularly those struggling with PTSD and suicidal ideation. The research highlights the therapeutic potential of equine-assisted interventions, most recently known as Equine Assisted Services (EAS), in supporting this underserved population.

The connection between horses and humans, particularly veterans, can be very powerful and often has a profound and lasting impact. Horses may be the thing that allows for the much-needed first step toward the release of pent-up or blocked emotions. The funny thing about horses is that they really are toddler-like, yet possess a wisdom that seems as old as time. Wise and discerning old man is one way to describe a gelding. Spunky and frat-boy-like is another more common way. Most types of horses are incredibly healing, with the ever-present potential for two scoops of entertainment and a possible side of major inconvenience.

Goose and Paul

Listed below are some key points about the special somatic (body-based) connection that has been known to develop between horses and veterans:

Nonverbal Communication

Horses are highly attuned to nonverbal cues and body language. This allows for a deep, nonverbal connection to develop as veterans interact with horses. Simply being next to a horse will often pull tears from an unsuspecting veteran, especially those new to horses. The release of tears is so important in the overall healing process.

Mirroring and Regulation

Horses can mirror the emotional states of humans. This can help veterans regulate their own emotions and physiological responses through the horse's calm presence. A horse will let out a long breath to signal a human to remember to breathe. Many humans approach horses in a dysregulated state. Horses see this as incongruence. The outside of the human may not match the inside. Someone with a big smile may be internally in a cortisol-flooded, permanent fight-or-flight state. Most humans are stuck in the sympathetic (fight-or-flight) state.

Sensory Awareness

Interacting with horses engages multiple senses: sight, sound, touch, smell, and... sometimes taste (sadly). This heightened sensory awareness can help veterans become more grounded in the present moment. They may note that everything is absolutely okay, right here and now. Continued episodes of everything being absolutely okay, right here and now, eventually allow for more ongoing peace of mind.

Somatic Resonance

The physical presence and movement of the horse can create a somatic resonance, allowing veterans to connect with their own bodies and physical experiences in a therapeutic way. The effects of these experiences have been known to provide more healing than one could ever imagine.

Trust and Safety

Horses are often seen as non-judgmental and provide a safe space for veterans to open up emotionally. This can facilitate the development of trust and allow the chance for the vets to be vulnerable, which means they are doing something significantly different and ultimately positive.

Autonomy and Mastery

Caring for and working with horses can help veterans regain a sense of autonomy and mastery, which will foster a feeling of empowerment and boost self-confidence. Horses seriously boost mood and hope. It is their inherent nature to be that for us.

Congressman Andy Barr (KY-06) has been known to advocate for various issues, including those related to veterans' mental health. One of the notable aspects of his work has involved promoting the therapeutic benefits of horses for veterans dealing with mental health challenges, such as PTSD and worse—frequent thoughts of hopelessness and suicide.

Barr has often highlighted programs that utilize Equine Assisted Services as a means of providing support and healing to veterans. He believes that interactions with horses can help reduce stress, improve emotional well-being, and facilitate social connections, which are crucial for veterans adjusting to civilian life. We love that he supports the unanimous U.S. House of Representatives vote in favor of S.785 - Commander John Scott Hannon Veterans Mental Health Care Improvement Act.

His statements typically emphasize the importance of addressing mental health issues among veterans and recognizing innovative approaches, like EAS, that can make a positive impact on their lives. By advocating for such programs, Barr aims to raise awareness and garner support for initiatives that provide essential services to those who have served in the military.

Interacting with horses requires individuals to be present and mindful, helping them to focus on the moment rather than their worries or reminders of their pasts. This mindfulness practice can benefit mental health recovery in ways we don't yet fully comprehend, though ongoing research shows promising developments, as does research on the vagus nerve.

Group sessions often include multiple participants, fostering social interaction and helping individuals develop communication and teamwork skills. Regarding veterans, the familiar camaraderie and easy interaction unfold in the presence of a horse.

Specifically, in the instance of vets with PTSD or trauma histories, the non-judgmental nature of horses can create a safe space to explore and process traumatic experiences.

CHAPTER 13

THE ART OF PAIRING HUMANS WITH HORSES

NOT ALL HORSES CAN BE RIDDEN BY BEGINNERS

"A horse is the projection of peoples' dreams about themselves–strong, powerful, beautiful–and it has the capability of giving us escape from our mundane existence." –Pam Brown.

One important job often goes unnoticed in a busy lesson barn bustling with activity. It's that of staff entrusted with pairing humans with horses for riding lessons. This chapter covers what this process entails and why it matters in ensuring a meaningful and safe learning experience.

The Science Behind Horse Assignment

Horse assignments may seem random to an outsider, but they're far from it. Many factors go into making these decisions, including the rider's skill level, physical attributes like height and weight, temperament compatibility between horse and human, and specific learning goals for each session.

For instance, if someone is taking their first-ever ride or is still getting comfortable around horses, they might be paired with a calm and patient horse known for its gentle nature and slower movement. These equine teachers are often older horses who have seen it all before. Common horse temperament descriptions may be listed as follows:

1. Calm/Quiet

2. More Whoa than Go

3. Not Spooky

4. Puppy Dog Horse

5. In Your Pocket Horse

6. Fill in Horse

7. Bomb Proof

8. Husband Horse

On the other hand, experienced riders aiming to refine advanced skills such as jumping or dressage could be matched with a more spirited horse that can challenge them while providing valuable feedback via subtle shifts in movement or behavior. A faster horse is known as a more "forward" horse.

Visualize this scene: You're standing at the edge of a paddock watching horses frolic freely. Some are lively, prancing around, while others quietly graze on a sunny patch. Each horse possesses unique characteristics that make it the perfect partner for different types of riders. A ballet dancer wouldn't wear football boots, after all! Marathon runners shouldn't wear combat boots 🧦 as a rule, and yet many do so to compete in the Boston Marathon.

Assigning an appropriate horse to each rider involves careful consideration based on several factors, such as skill level and temperament compatibility, ensuring both safety and progression in learning.

A Fun Twist

Remember playing musical chairs? Horse assignment can sometimes feel similar. As new students come in and existing ones advance or change their learning goals, the dance of horse-rider pairing continues. It's a dynamic process that keeps everyone on their toes–literally!

What to Do When the Problem Seems Extra Hard

Sometimes, despite careful planning, a horse-rider pair might click differently than expected. It could be an energy mismatch or a bad day for either party. In such cases, it's crucial to offer immediate support and, if necessary, switch horses to confirm safety and comfort for both rider and horse.

Avoiding Common Pitfalls

One common mistake is rushing this process or neglecting its importance–a critical point for parents of riders to remember. Assigning horses based on special requests (like the color of a horse or its pretty mane) can lead to frustrated riders or stressed horses, which hinders the overall progress.

Understanding Why Horse Assignment Matters

Let's imagine you're learning salsa dancing but paired with a partner who only knows ballet–it would be restricting at best and disastrous at worst! Probably pretty hilarious to watch, though. Like dance partners, matching the right horse with the right human makes all the difference in ensuring smooth sailing (or riding).

———

Point to Ponder:

• Pairing humans with horses isn't random; it involves assessing several factors.

• Understanding individual characteristics of each horse and rider is crucial.

• The process should be dynamic and flexible based on changing needs.

• Immediate intervention is necessary when a pair doesn't work out.

• Neglecting this aspect can hinder progress in lessons and cause huge frustration for both horse and rider.

Remember that, like any good relationship, finding the perfect horse-human match may take time–but once found, it paves the way for an enriching journey filled with growth and connection. So, next time you see someone working behind the scenes assigning horses in your lesson barn, give them a nod of recognition–they're playing cupid in one of the most beautiful dances between man and beast! This will ensure the best experience for your child and their four-legged partner.

Chapter 14

Navigating the Equestrian World: Selecting Your Equestrian Style

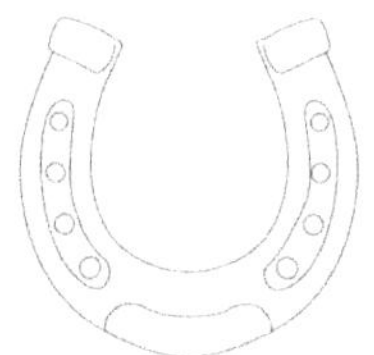

The world of horse riding is vast and diverse. From Western riding with its cowboy roots and boots to the elegance of Hunter/Jumper and Dressage, there's no shortage of styles to choose from. But don't let this overwhelm you. As Sally Swift emphasized in her book *Centered Riding,* fundamentals remain constant regardless of what type of riding you do.

Firstly, it's important to understand that each style has its unique strengths and requirements, both physically and financially.

Let's start with Western riding. Imagine galloping through open fields with nothing but the wind against your face. Exciting, isn't it? Originating from cattle work on ranches in America's Wild West, this style favors comfort and practicality over formality. The saddles are designed for day-long rides and include a horn at the front for roping cattle. In terms of monetary investment, Western riding can be less expensive as it requires fewer accessories than other styles. Western best meets your initial needs if you have always dreamed of being a cowboy or cowgirl.

Dressage or classical English riding (Hunter/Jumper) is often compared to ballet on horseback because of its emphasis on gracefulness and precision. The rider communicates their commands through subtle movements that must be executed perfectly by the horse. Think "Swan Lake" meets Kentucky Derby! However, bear in mind that dressage requires specific equipment like dress boots and breeches, which can add up quickly. And I do mean quickly! Really. Insanely quickly.

Pro Tip: Ask for receipts and paper proof when dealing with anyone horse-related. It is tough to prove or know the value or history of most horses.

There are other disciplines to explore, too: Working Equitation (see the next chapter for more info), Grand Prix, and Eventing, to name just a few.

Now, let's address a common misconception. Does the type of riding really matter? The answer is yes... and no. Yes, because each style has unique techniques requiring different skills and tack. No, because the fundamental principles of good horsemanship–balance, rhythm, and harmony–apply to all styles. The fundamentals of riding remain the same.

Stay as balanced and centered as you can, and your movements will flow with the horse as one.

So, how do you choose? Start by trying out different styles. Most equestrian centers offer trial lessons for beginners where you can get a feel for each discipline before committing to one. Consider factors like your physical fitness level, budget, and personal preferences when making your decision.

Remember that becoming proficient in any riding style takes practice and patience, so don't rush it. Like mastering an instrument or learning a new language, it's less about reaching an end goal and more about enjoying the journey. Do you know how many times I have personally been fed that last line? Thousands.

If you struggle with choosing a discipline or facing difficulties in mastering it, take heart! Many great riders have faced similar challenges but persevered through sheer determination and love for these magnificent creatures. Oh–and there's the mildly obsessive addiction part, too. Seriously.

One young rider here at Salko Farm told her mother after her 30-minute lesson, "I am always so sad when I leave Salko Farm." Her mother said, "Well, I guess the half-hour lesson is not really long enough." Her daughter responded, "You don't understand. I'm sad about leaving Salko Farm even after a full week of camp. I *never* want to leave there."

CHAPTER 15

NEWEST AND FASTEST GROWING EQUINE SPORT: WORKING EQUITATION COMPETITION

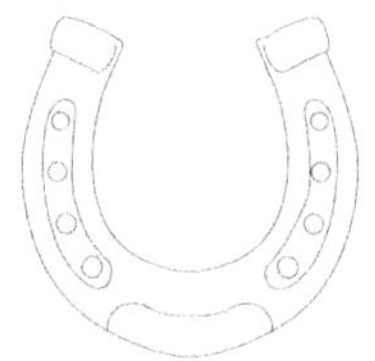

Welcome to the exciting world of working equitation. This relatively fresh and fast-growing equestrian sport is gaining popularity all over the globe. It's a unique blend of dressage, obstacle course riding, and speed work that tests both horse and rider's agility, precision, and teamwork skills.

These phases are designed to test your horse's versatility and obedience while showcasing your skill as a rider.

Working equitation originated in Europe to display the versatile abilities required from horses used for fieldwork in various countries. The aim was to showcase not only their athleticism but also their ability to stay calm under pressure while performing tasks that would be common on a farm or ranch setting. This makes it an ideal sport for those who enjoy endurance rides or trail riding.

Many successful riders have shared their experiences about their journey into this sport. For instance, Pedro Torres, the 2008 World Champion, began his career focusing on traditional dressage before falling in love with working equitation at his first competition.

Analyzing working equitation reveals its uniqueness across many dimensions: It celebrates cultural diversity by embracing different styles of horsemanship worldwide, promotes versatility in horses, and emphasizes harmony between horse and rider above all else.

Additionally, this multidisciplinary approach reduces the risk of injuries compared with more specialized equestrian sports–specifically jumping.

Case studies from scientific research papers show that working equitation can positively impact both horse and rider. A study published in the Journal of Equine Veterinary Science found that horses participating in this sport had increased core strength and improved balance, while riders reported enhanced communication skills with their horses. A significant bond occurs due to the task-specific elements of this sport. Horse and rider work together with such a joint purpose that the overall value and feeling of worthiness (especially for the horse) are powerful and proven. Overall, general riding efficiency is improved.

———

Points to Ponder:

• It originated in Europe but has grown internationally.

• The sport tests the versatility, obedience, and athleticism of the horse and the skill of the rider. Great connection and teamwork are required.

• Working equitation is open to all types of horses, not just specific breeds or sizes!

To get started on your path with working equitation:

1. Familiarize yourself: Learn its history, rules, scoring system, etc.

2. Find a coach: An experienced coach will guide you through training your horse.

3. Join a local club: Participate in local events for practice before entering competitions.

4. Equipment check: Ensure you have suitable tack (saddle, bridle) suitable for dressage and obstacle course riding.

5. Regular practice: Consistent training sessions will help build up your confidence and skills over time. This is a relatively new sport. It is evolving and growing regularly with specific and detailed changes to the rules and regulations. Watch carefully if you intend to compete. Thankfully, the sport is well-standardized and has healthy and varied competition.

Advanced riders who are already familiar with basic aspects of this sport should consider attending clinics led by top competitors or judges to hone their skills further. Participate regularly in local competitions to gain experience and exposure. Consider investing in a horse bred for working equitation if you're serious about competing at high levels.

Remember, the pathway to mastering working equitation requires time, dedication, and, above all, patience. The joy is not just in winning but also in developing a strong and loving relationship with your horse. Maybe not quite as exciting as Pickle Ball taking the world by storm, still exciting all the same.

CHAPTER 16

THE PERFECT PASTURE: FINDING THE RIGHT LESSON BARN

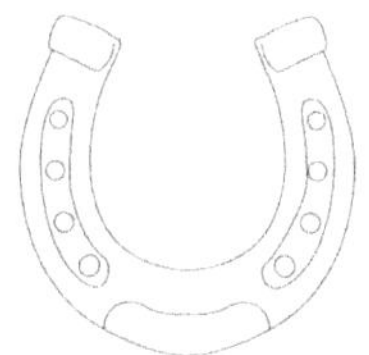

When raising a child with an equestrian passion, you might feel like you're not just parenting a toddler but also caring for a 1,200-pound bundle of joy. It's akin to standing at the edge of a large prairie with no map or compass, with your child's happiness and safety on the line. NO WATER and no snacks. But fear not! This chapter will serve as your GPS in navigating this unknown and mysterious terrain.

First: Not all horse-riding schools are created equal. They're as different as apples and oranges–or should we say Shetland ponies and thorough-breds? Or hacks vs. professionals.

The starting point is understanding what you need from a lesson barn. Is it proximity? Professional trainers? Or perhaps it's about that elusive "vibe" that makes your child's eyes light up brighter than sparklers on the 4th of July.

In my opinion, until the rider has narrowed down their number of sports to horseback riding and maybe one other, the trainer won't matter much. Changing trainers is usually a good thing so that the kids are taught by different styles of trainers. With the youngest kids, it is about keeping the instructor/trainer the same for comfort with shyness.

Now comes the fun part–research! With our modern-day oracle, Google, by your side, start scanning for local stables. Look for reviews: They're like secret whispers from other parents guiding you toward or away from certain places. Though obviously, discount the scathers who you know leave a similarly toned review for most people she deals with daily. 😄

Of course, we are sometimes forced to cross paths with disgruntled and disruptive people. Some people are only happy if they are complaining. We can imagine that some things have happened to them along the way to make them feel angry and somewhat alone against the world. Horses help the "closed-off" and guarded people let their guards down. If that happens, we are able to find our authentic, softer, and more vulnerable sides.

Recommended Steps:

When picking out a riding school, think of yourself as Goldilocks testing out porridge bowls–look until you find one that's "just right."

The next step is visiting potential barns–yes, plural! Think of them like houses; would you buy one without touring several others first? As Einstein wisely observed, "The only source of knowledge is experience." So, roll up those sleeves and schedule some tours.

A well-managed barn should be clean enough to make Mary Poppins nod in approval (or at least not cause her to faint or do that tutting thing that she did). A strong odor or disheveled appearance can indicate poor management–amongst other things, you might want to look into further. Safety should be paramount, so check for emergency procedures clearly displayed and first aid kits easily accessible. Does the facility have a State Law Equestrian Sport sign visibly posted? Are the instructors certified by any official riding instructor organization? These are all things that should exist, or the lesson facility should be avoided.

Check out the horses themselves. They should be well-groomed and their stalls clean, dry, and spacious. A happy horse is a healthy horse, and that's exactly what you want your child to learn with. (Or yourself, especially if you are approaching brittle bone chapters in your life as I am.)

The staff are vital, too; they're the people who will guide your child on this journey. Are they qualified? Experienced? Do they have a soft spot for kids? You wouldn't trust just anyone to teach your child math, would you?

If the barn checks all these boxes but something still feels off, trust your gut–it's usually right. There's that intuition showing up again. Trust it —it's the true you!

Now, let's address the elephant in the room: COST. Horse riding isn't cheap but remember: You're investing not only in lessons but in life skills like responsibility, discipline, accountability, and compassion.

Finally, if things get really tough, like there aren't any suitable barns nearby, or costs are prohibitive, consider alternatives like sharing a horse or looking into pony clubs that can offer similar benefits at a reduced price.

In summary:

• Know what you need from a lesson barn.

• Research local stables and look for reviews.

• Visit potential barns to gauge cleanliness, safety measures, condition of horses, and qualifications of staff.

• Trust your instincts.

• Consider cost as an investment in life skills and well-being for your children or yourself. Therapy type investment.

• Look into alternatives, if needed. Consider resources for other forms of personal growth and development.

Remember, fellow parent navigators, finding the right lesson barn might feel like searching for a needle in a haystack (quite literally), but when you see your child beaming atop their equine partner under an azure sky, every effort will prove worth it! With Google reviews and more, you are more likely to find a good fit than you used to be when researching this type of thing. **Take it seriously. Due to the nature of the horse world and the fact that it is not well-governed or standardized, more caution is needed when researching it than when researching other, more regulated activities for children.**

CHAPTER 17

HORSE BARN AND ARENA RIDING ETIQUETTE

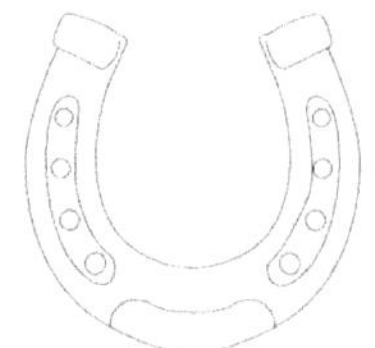

When it comes to the world of equestrianism, the environment in which we ride and care for our horses is just as important as the skills we develop in the saddle. Understanding and practicing proper etiquette in the horse barn and riding arena not only enhances the experience for everyone involved but also fosters a spirit of community and respect among riders, trainers, and horses alike. We will explore essential guidelines for ensuring a safe and enjoyable atmosphere in both settings.

The Horse Barn: A Sanctuary for Horses and Riders (the crazier the owner, the more rules to follow).

The horse barn is more than just a shelter; it is a sanctuary where horses are cared for, and riders bond with their equine partners. Respecting this space begins with recognizing the unique needs of both the horses and the people who work with them.

1. Quiet and Calm Environment: Horses are sensitive creatures, and loud noises or sudden movements can startle (spook) them. Speak softly when inside the barn and avoid running or making abrupt gestures. This calm atmosphere helps keep the horses relaxed and content. Think "Tai-Chi" slow.

2. Respect Personal Space: Each horse has its own comfort zone. When approaching a horse, always do so from the side, allowing them to see you coming. Avoid standing directly behind them, as this is their blind spot and can lead to unintended accidents. Well, unintended for humans, for sure. The horse—questionable. 😊

3. Cleaning Up After Yourself: Whether you are grooming, feeding, or simply visiting, always clean up after yourself. This includes putting away tools, disposing of any trash, and ensuring that the aisle is clear of obstacles. A tidy barn is a safe barn. All tack should be cleaned and put back in its place!

4. Handling Equipment with Care: Horse equipment, from saddles to bridles, is often expensive and can be easily damaged. Always return items to their proper place after use and handle them gently to avoid wear and tear. Always label your equipment. You'd be amazed (or maybe not) at how many little Suzies have left a $300 helmet without a name on it. Many, many, many.

5. Be Mindful of Others: There may be multiple people working in the barn at once. Be aware of your surroundings and avoid blocking entrances or exits. If you see someone struggling with a task, offer assistance if you can.

The Riding Arena: A Shared Space for Learning and Growth

The riding arena is a dynamic environment where riders of all skill levels come together to train, compete, and enjoy their time with horses. Proper etiquette in the arena is crucial to ensure safety and foster a supportive community.

1. Know the Rules: Every riding facility may have its own rules regarding arena use. Please familiarize yourself with these guidelines, whether they pertain to riding direction, jump placement, or time limits for usage. You will often see a barn sign saying, "MY BARN, MY RULES!" This sign means business–please adhere at all times. A barn owner will typically be a stickler for rules, as this is how the entire establishment is kept safe and user-friendly.

2. Observe Before You Ride: Before entering the arena, take a moment to observe the current activities. Are there riders jumping, practicing dressage, or free lunging? Understanding what others are doing helps you plan your practice without disrupting theirs.

3. Communicate Clearly: Clear communication is key when riding in a group. Use vocal cues or hand signals to indicate your intentions, such as when passing another rider or transitioning to a different gait. This helps prevent accidents and keeps everyone informed. "On your left" is one such cue to let another rider know you are coming up on their left or passing them on the left.

4. Maintain a Safe Distance: Always keep a safe distance between your horse and others. This prevents collisions and allows each horse to feel secure in its space. If riding in a smaller arena, be especially mindful of your proximity to others. Many horses have issues with other horses. It is always best to keep at least a horse-length distance between any two horses—much more than that if the space is available.

Prince, Snip, and Paul 🤍

5. Be Considerate of Time: If you are practicing a specific skill, be aware of how long you are occupying the arena, especially during busy times. Consider sharing the space, allowing others a turn, or moving to a less crowded area for more focused practice.

6. Help and Encourage Others: Equestrian pursuits can be challenging. Some people may not realize how technical and specific the movements and theories of horseback riding can be. Add to that that horses are typically moody and easily distracted, and you can only imagine how some of these frustrating combos show up in the ring. There are often many different levels of riders in an arena at any one time. Offer encouragement to fellow riders and be willing to share tips or advice when asked. A supportive atmosphere enhances everyone's experience.

Etiquette in the horse barn and riding arena is about more than just following rules; it is about cultivating respect, safety, and camaraderie within the equestrian community. By adhering to these guidelines, riders enhance their own experiences and contribute positively to the environment around them. As we continue to grow in our skills and relationships with our horses, let us remember the importance of etiquette as we create a harmonious space for all.

I feel like I need to stress this again. The horse world is dominated by females with moxie! Moxie and strong opinions, let's say.

The horses enhance these intuitive senses in us and it is always in our best interests to obey those signals. "Take heed," I believe is a phrase used "back in the day."

CHAPTER 18

THE ART OF GROOMING AND TACKING

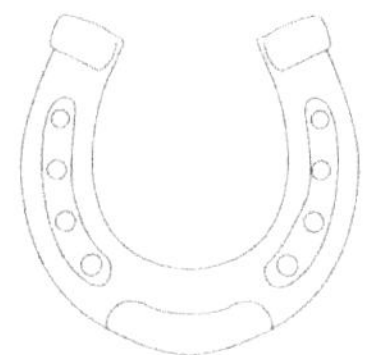

Grooming and tacking are essential skills in equestrianism that can significantly enhance your relationship with your horse. It's about more than just cleanliness; it's valuable bonding time, a health check-up, and preparation for either work or play.

Let's start with grooming. Imagine walking into an art gallery filled with immaculate sculptures, their polished surfaces gleaming under the spotlights. Your horse is like one of these sculptures–majestic, powerful, beautiful–and it deserves to be treated as such.

Grooming is an art form in itself. With each stroke of the brush, you're not only removing dirt but also massaging your horse's skin, increasing blood flow, and maintaining his overall health. Most horses love being groomed. Plus, this routine provides an opportunity to check for abnormalities like bumps or cuts that might need attention.

There is also a science behind effective grooming. Researchers from the University of Minnesota found that regular grooming can significantly reduce stress levels in horses. So, next time you lift your brush, think of it as a magic wand dispersing calmness! The same is true for people! Anxiety levels in humans are reduced drastically and with lasting and multiple benefits when grooming horses.

Pro Tip:

Some people clean hooves first. Some start by using a curry comb in circular motions to loosen dirt and dead hair, then follow up with soft brushes to remove it. A grooming ritual should be loosely followed to ensure the horses are correctly readied to be ridden.

Now, let's move on to tacking up, another essential skill every rider must master. Imagine dressing up for a formal event; each piece has its place, contributing to perfection. (I personally can NOT imagine that, as it is my worst nightmare to dress up for anything other than country line-dancing... meaning fancier boots, with fancier jeans!) The same goes for tacking, but we need to learn new vocabulary before that happens.

Choosing the right tack could mean the difference between winning or losing at dressage events or overall safety during working equitation and any other form of training sessions. More importantly, though, it affects comfort levels for both horse and rider, directly impacting performance and the overall bond of horse and rider.

For example, an ill-fitted saddle can cause discomfort, leading to behavioral problems in horses and back pain in riders over time—definitely not what we want!

"A well-fitted saddle is worth its weight in gold." –Unknown

Let's compare the importance of tacking to wearing a pair of shoes. If they're too tight or loose, you'll end up with sore feet and an awkward gait, which could lead to more serious issues down the line. Also, think about those bunions you may develop over time, with overuse of those high-heeled shoes. The same principle applies to horses–their tack needs to be just right! This includes their shoes... in fact, shoes are the most important. If a horse is missing one shoe–one of either, two total, or four total shoes–that horse should *not* be ridden. Balance is everything to horses and their riders.

Consider consulting a professional saddle fitter if your horse is extra sensitive or has had previous injuries. They can provide custom solutions that will ensure comfort and performance.

To wrap it all up, let's summarize:

- Grooming isn't just about cleanliness; it's a bonding activity that promotes health and well-being, for both horse and rider.
- Regular grooming can reduce stress levels in horses and riders. This is huge.
- Tack must fit correctly for the comfort and performance of both horse and rider.
- When in doubt, talk to professionals. Ask more than one person from different sources. The horse world really needs many cross-checks and safety nets for cynicism and corruption.

Sadly, the horse world is full of unqualified people spouting nonsense. I mean this, and I will give you an example.

While attending a rather reputable organization's weekend workshop, whose work is followed by an Ivy League school, I encountered one of their staff members teaching new horse people that a currycomb (usually round or oval in shape) was to be used in line with the horse's hair. That is absolutely not correct.

This little detail came from a friend and weekly rider at Salko Farm, who came to me for clarification on currycombs after being told the above by a facilitator of this workshop.

How does someone tactfully handle that? I will tell you what I did—tactful is not a typical adjective for me—but I will go with what I did and you can let me know.

The next morning, we were in groups, grooming. I chose to groom the horse held by the lady who did not know how to use a currycomb properly. From there, I wasn't sure what to do. Then I got it. I picked up a currycomb, a round one, held it high in the air, and asked the group director, "Hey Susie, the currycomb goes in a circle, to get the dirt to the surface, right? The woman holding the horse, who I was standing beside, started to say, "No," and the director yelled out, "Yes, a currycomb goes in a circle." Sad and true story. Embarassing, but also potentially dangerous in a different scenario.

Check your facts and ask for written proof whenever possible. If you Google search professionals, look for reviews and comments to gauge their credibility and effectiveness. Take what you find with a grain of salt until you've verified the source as reputable.

Remember this chapter the next time you approach grooming and tacking as mundane tasks–they're much more than that! These are the moments when bonds are formed, health is promoted, comfort is ensured, and performances are enhanced. Your horses thrive on good grooming.

To Tack Just One Horse

Just to tack one horse, you need to know the length of the rider's legs and the rider's ability before you even know which horse to tack. The horse is graded in terms of advancement, temperament, and size.

The size of the saddle–weird measurement–not even going to try to describe it. It's a little like the hands of horses, except not at all. I am a size 17—and that's not as bad as it looks on paper.

The size of the girth (or cinch if Western)–it can't be too tight and it can't be too loose–Goldilocks' just right is the ticket!

Both saddle pad and sheepskin pad? Just a saddle pad? Gel pad? Extra padding at the withers?

What type of bit, bridle, single reins, double reins, one rein, two reins?

Does the horse need a martingale? A standing martingale or a running martingale? And if you forget your horse Milo's martingale one day, just sayin', you may end up eating dirt with a fat lip and a bruised ego.

Chapter 19

When Will I Canter?

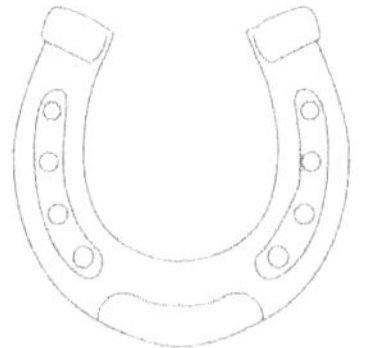

One question that might come up is, "How long will it take me to canter?" This chapter considers this very aspect, unraveling the layers of complexities involved in mastering the canter and how to navigate through them.

Cantering is a beautiful symphony between the rider and the horse, an intricate dance that needs harmony, understanding, and patience. It's not just about getting on a horse; it's about building a relationship with these incredible creatures. Before we explore further, let's peel back some more layers.

First, remember that each individual's journey toward mastering the canter is unique. Factors like age, fitness level, confidence, and comfort around horses all play crucial roles in determining how quickly one can learn to canter successfully. Instructors often feel pressure from parents of young riders, which is unacceptable. Parents often want their children to achieve milestones quickly, which may not always be conducive to learning at a natural pace. Accidents occur when things like cantering are rushed. I cannot stress this enough... the best instructors out there will take the longest time to prepare your child for safely cantering. I liken it to learning to drive - only on a horse there is no seatbelt or metal frame around you, like you have in a car. When you first learn to drive it is parking lots and then side streets. The last thing you do, once you've mastered all the controls, buttons, steering, and personality of your car/**horse**–is add speed and hit the highway/**canter**. We walk before we run. Cantering takes body strength and control, along with strong confidence, and there should be a feeling that you move with your horse as one.

Furthermore, lesson horses are great teachers, but they also have limitations. They're often older or less fit than other horses; dealing with beginner riders can lead them to develop habits that aren't beneficial for learning correct techniques. A lesson horse has learned to "fill in" for their riders. They pretend to understand exactly what their little rider wants through the ambiguity of a newer rider's instructions. A non-lesson horse will respond as a horse should. *I have no idea what you want from me, and that's scary, so let's just go! Let's run from the real issue here... I am terrified. I will throw my hooves in the air due to the presence of this clueless and directionless human (predator) on my prey-like back*—cue eyeroll. Seriously, think of Renaldo or Rooney–one of those famous footballers (soccer players)–the over-dramatization of a little trip–the horse is all about that type of grandstanding. (I mention this again as I do love a good run-on joke. I love English football!)

Now, on to our main content—developing your cantering skills. Your first steps will involve gaining balance and control at slower gaits: walk and trot. You need to build muscle memory before moving on to faster gaits like cantering.

Pro Tip: Patience pays off when learning to ride!

Many studies support this claim, showing that gradual progression leads to better skill retention in equestrian sports.

Consider the story of Amelia Henley, who began riding lessons as an adult with no prior experience around horses. Her trainer started her off slowly, focusing on basic horsemanship skills before she moved on to more advanced ones like cantering. It took her a year to canter comfortably, but the wait was worth it. She now competes in dressage and jumping events.

Riding horses isn't just about learning specific skills; it's about the journey and enjoying each moment spent with your equine partner.

Analyzing these facets further, one realizes that physical readiness is only half the battle won. Mental preparedness for cantering is equally important. Fear or overexcitement could lead to incorrect cues, confusing your horse. The ambiguity problem rears its ugly head. Clear and concise works best. Consistency is key with both toddlers and horses.

I read and lived by Barbara Colaroso's book *Kids Are Worth It*. It is an incredibly effective and easy way to parent, and the information in it is invaluable. If you are a parent, you must read this book.

You might want to jot this down:

• Make sure you're physically ready before attempting to canter. This means months of leg and core strengthening exercises. We have included a short chapter covering the best riding-specific training exercises.

• Develop a strong relationship with your horse. The simplest way to do this is to spend time near your horse in silence.

• Overcoming fear and anxiety plays a big role in successful cantering.

When smaller children are involved, ensure the strength level is available. Core and leg strength are needed to support this faster gait. This is serious. A rider should be able to post the trot without stirrups for at least one lap of the riding arena, a clear sign that the rider has the adductor strength to better stay on the horse should the rider "lose their stirrup."

Speaking of adductors... here's another example of fraud in the horse world. An ex-instructor of Salko Farm arranged for an expensive workshop to be held here at the farm. I was in attendance when the expensive workshop facilitator woman pointed to her inner thighs and described needing to strengthen their *ab*ductors. Ummm, so I asked "*AB*ductor? Or adductor?"

"A B ductor," she said.

I was embarrassed for her. Get this—no one else in attendance knew any better. So, the horse world is a place to tread carefully.

According to equestrian statistics, about 70% of riders report experiencing fear or anxiety at some stage, which obviously affects their riding progress. Overcoming mental barriers speeds up the learning process! Anxiety in riders isn't uncommon–overcoming it makes all the difference!

To achieve a smooth transition into canter:

• First, build up your confidence and balance at slower gaits.

• Learn to give correct aids consistently.

• Spend more time around horses to understand them better.

• Work on overcoming any fears related to riding.

Years of experience within this arena show that patience, consistent practice, and, most importantly, enjoying the process are what make this journey truly rewarding! Remaining both fluid and flexible is key.

CHAPTER 20

5 BEST RIDING SPECIFIC EXERCISES:

BUILDING STRENGTH AND STAMINA FOR HORSEBACK RIDING

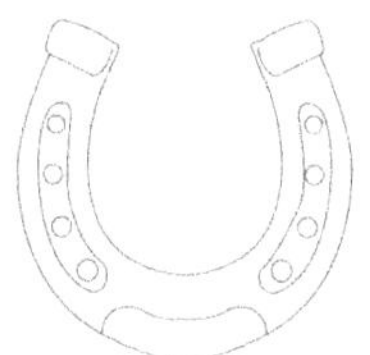

Horseback riding is a multifaceted sport that requires not only skill but also significant physical conditioning. You may think your thighs are colossally strong. That thought will no longer be present once you've spent 30 minutes in the saddle! 😄😄😄 Riders must utilize various muscle groups to maintain balance, control, and stamina throughout their rides. Understanding the specific muscle strength required for effective riding can help riders train more effectively. This chapter will explore the essential muscle groups used during riding and provide the top five exercises to enhance strength and stamina.

Different muscle groups play critical roles in supporting balance and control while riding, each contributing to the rider's ability to maintain a secure and effective position in the saddle.

Here's a breakdown of how various muscle groups work together to enhance balance and control:

1. Core Muscles

Role: The core muscles, including the abdominals, obliques, and lower back, provide stability and support to the spine.

Function: A strong core helps riders maintain an upright position and absorb the horse's movements. This stability allows for better weight distribution, essential for effective communication with the horse. Horses like as little extra movement (or wiggling) as possible. The more control you have of your core, the more quietly you will hold your body on top of any horse.

2. Leg Muscles

Role: The quadriceps, hamstrings, calves, and hip flexors are vital for leg positioning and control.

Function: Strong legs enable riders to create effective leg aids, maintain a secure grip on the horse, and adjust their position as needed. The ability to flex and extend the legs helps balance and shift weight effectively. Again, the more fine motor movement control you have over both the upper and lower parts of the leg, the better. This control comes from having good overall strength. Control of the smaller, more specific muscles only comes once the larger groups have been conditioned.

Harley

3. Back Muscles

Role: The muscles in the back, including the latissimus dorsi, trapezius, and spinal erectors, support the upper body's posture.

Function: A strong back allows for better upper body control, preventing slumping or leaning that can disrupt balance. It also helps maintain a strong connection with the horse through the reins.

4. Shoulder and Arm Muscles

Role: The shoulders, biceps, triceps, and forearms are crucial for controlling the reins and guiding the horse.

Function: Strong shoulders and arms stabilize the upper body, allowing for precise movements and adjustments without compromising balance. This ensures that the rider remains centered and can effectively communicate with the horse. "Smooth" and "flowing" are two words you would like to have associated with how your arms move beside your body. Your elbow and shoulder joints soak up the bounce to keep that much-needed constant contact with the bit, the reins, and your gently flowing arms and hands. Again, *Centered Riding* by Sally Swift is the best foundations book.

5. Hip Muscles

Role: The hip flexors and gluteal muscles support leg movement and stability.

Function: Strong hips allow for a better range of motion and flexibility, which is important for adjusting weight distribution and maintaining balance during various riding maneuvers, such as posting or transitioning between gaits.

6. Ankle and Foot Muscles

Role: Calf and intrinsic foot muscles aid the rider's stability in the stirrups. Pressing down solidly at the very back edge of the ball of your foot allows for great leg steadiness and contact on the horse. Sally Swift of Centered Riding fame suggested that the perfect ball for foot placement is called the "bubbling spring."

Function: Strong ankles and feet help riders maintain a secure position in the saddle and provide a stable base for leg aids. This stability is crucial for effective communication with the horse and overall balance.

Together, these muscle groups work in harmony to provide the balance and control required for horseback riding. A well-conditioned rider can maintain a centered position, respond quickly to the horse's movements, and execute precise aids, ultimately leading to a more harmonious partnership with their equine companion. Regular strength training and conditioning exercises targeting these muscle groups can significantly enhance a rider's performance and overall riding experience.

Top 5 Exercises for Strength and Stamina in Riding

1. Planks

Muscle Groups Targeted: Core, shoulders, back, glutes, quadriceps, and chest.

How to Perform: Start in a push-up position with your arms straight and body in a straight line from head to heels. Hold this position for 30 seconds to a minute, gradually increasing the duration as you build strength. Variations include side planks or planks with leg lifts to challenge stability.

Plank, plank, plank, plank, plank. Slowly building your plank hold time to something like four minutes will help you produce a rock-solid core!

2. Squats

Muscle Groups Targeted: Legs, core, glutes

How to Perform: Stand with feet shoulder-width apart. Lower your body as if sitting back into a chair, keeping your knees over your toes and chest up. Go as low as comfortable, then push through the four corners of your feet to return to standing. Aim for three sets of 10-15 repetitions. *Please do not* allow your knees to come forward of your toes. This is a bad way to treat your knees.

3. Deadlifts

Muscle Groups Targeted: Back, legs, core

How to Perform: Stand with feet hip-width apart, holding a barbell or dumbbell in front of your thighs. With a slight bend in your knees, hinge (bend forward) at your hips to lower the weights down your legs, keeping your back straight. Return to standing by keeping your weight in your heels. Aim for three sets of 8-10 repetitions.

4. Wall Sits or Sitting in Infinity

Muscle Groups Targeted: Glutes, quads, hamstrings, calves, and core

How to Perform: Stand with your feet hip-width (or slightly wider) apart.

Strength and stamina are essential for any horseback rider looking to improve their performance. Focusing on the key muscle groups utilized during riding and incorporating targeted exercises into your training routine will enhance your riding capabilities. Consistent practice of these exercises will improve your physical fitness and contribute to a more enjoyable and effective riding experience. Remember to consult with a fitness professional or coach to ensure you are performing exercises correctly and safely.

CHAPTER 21

A Beginner's Guide to Equine Purchase

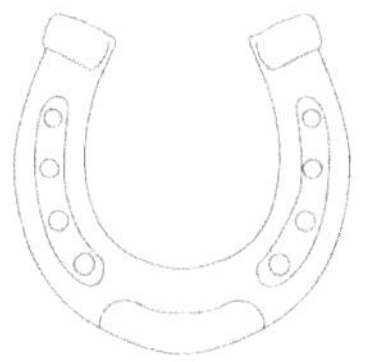

"Horse sense is the thing a horse has which keeps it from betting on people."
– W.C. Fields

The thrill of owning your first horse can be as intoxicating as a ride through an open meadow under a bright summer sky. But let's pause for a moment and step back from this picturesque fantasy. Buying a horse isn't all about galloping into sunsets; it involves thorough research, understanding, and some serious decision-making. Owning a horse is not for everyone and is unnecessary for horse-human connection experiences. Please beware of the persistence potential of a young child, now obsessed and compelled by these majestic equines. Their non-stop, downright professionally polished begging skills are to be admired when in the name of a horse.

Picture yourself at an equine auction or viewing horses online, each one more beautiful than the last. Beware! This is when you are likely to catch what equestrians call "barn blindness"–falling in love with every horse you see! It's like walking into a candy store with no adult supervision. Seriously, if there is a kryptonite for me–other than Sweet Tart Chewy Fusion–it is pretty much any horse (especially one with a sob story!) You must resist this temptation and make informed decisions based on facts rather than emotions. *Again*, you must resist this temptation and make informed decisions based on facts rather than emotions.

Always approach buying a horse with clear-headed practicality rather than emotional impulsivity. This statement is the equivalent of a full-blown oxymoron.

Let us explore the world of equine purchase and learn how to navigate the horse market maze.

First, we need to understand that there are three genders in horses: stallions (intact males), mares (females), and geldings (castrated males). If you're new to horsemanship, steer clear of stallions; they require experienced handling because of their testosterone-fueled behavior. Most lesson barns will not house them because of the potential risks involved.

Think, "Here's Johnny!" from *The Shining*–that's pretty much stallion behavior... psychotic and furious.

Geldings are generally calmer, while mares can be moodier owing to hormonal fluctuations. Think PMS women–it can be soooo big when this is happening in a horse-sized monthly dose!!! Right.

Horses have personalities like humans, intertwined with their pecking order within the herd hierarchy. Spend time observing prospective horses interacting with other animals and humans before deciding. You wouldn't buy a car without test-driving it, would you?

When buying a horse, you need to be aware of certain pitfalls and tricks of the trade.

Beware of sellers who are overly keen to sell or refuse vet checks. Remember, if something sounds too good to be true, it probably is! Especially with horses.

If you encounter an exceptionally problematic situation during your horse purchasing journey, consider seeking professional advice from experienced equestrians or reputable trainers in the field.

Let's now segue into the "aha" moment–understanding why some horses may have issues and how best to address them.

Horses can develop behavioral problems for various reasons, such as poor training methods, inappropriate handling, or underlying health issues.

Scotty

**The solution lies not in quick fixes but in understanding and
addressing these root causes correctly.
The same goes for people.**

For example, a horse that bucks frequently might not just be "spirited," as some might label him; he could be suffering from back pain or saddle discomfort. It could even be something like an ulcer.

Thus, buying a horse requires knowledge about equine behavior and health, apart from considering factors like age, breed, or color, such as any naughty horse habits they may have, like cribbing or weaving.

Summing Up an Equine Purchase:

1. Resist impulsive purchases based on emotions. Read this again. And again.

2. Understand that geldings and mares are preferable over stallions for beginners. In general, stallions are not the best option to choose as your riding partner.

3. Spend time observing a prospective horse's behavior before making decisions.

4. Be aware of common sales scams and remain cautious throughout the process.

5. Seek professional help when faced with complex situations.

6. Understand that behavioral issues often stem from underlying problems that require suitable action rather than quick fixes.

7. Is the horse on regular maintenance of injections, calming tablets, or other supplements—in order to be rideable?

Approach your first horse purchase with patience, diligence, and excitement!

CHAPTER 22

Unveiling the Hidden Costs and Unscrupulous Frauds in Horseback Riding

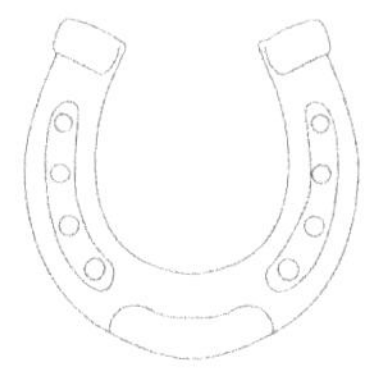

Horseback riding, a beautiful blend of artistry, athleticism, and animal connection, is alluring for many. However, the cost and potential pitfalls can be a nightmare for parents wanting to support their child's equestrian dreams. You might assume horseback riding is expensive and still be shocked at how costly it can become!

Historically, horses have been symbols of nobility and wealth. Today's equestrian world keeps some of this exclusivity. Each aspect comes with its price tag, from equipment to lessons to owning or leasing horses. However, knowing how to direct your money and what you're actually paying for is vital.

The most significant expense is usually the horse itself. Purchasing your own horse is a huge undertaking and should not be considered lightly. Leasing a horse may seem more affordable than buying one outright but scrutinizing whether the lease makes sense is crucial. Some stables may propose leasing arrangements that are more convenient for them than beneficial to you or your child. This is a serious issue in the horse world. If something seems fishy, it probably is, though in horse-sized proportions.

When considering a lease-horse match-up, check if the horse's size fits your child's stature properly. Don't let yourself get talked into an ill-suited arrangement just because it initially seems convenient or less expensive.

Be vigilant about evaluating lease arrangements against your child's needs. If your child is still growing, insist on the shorter lease agreement, six months at a time. You can half-lease a horse, too. These are options to be researched separately.

Harley the Love Bug

A lesson I learned from years of observing barns across various regions is that not everyone operates with integrity, and some people exploit the innocents' ignorance or passion for their own personal gain.

One common trick unscrupulous barns use involves recommending specific gear stores that sell overpriced items or frequently suggesting unnecessary equipment upgrades. Evidence supporting this assertion abounds in online forums, where parents share stories of being manipulated into making purchases they later regretted.

For instance, Jane Doe shared on the Equestrian Parents Anonymous forum about being persuaded to buy her daughter custom-made boots costing upward of $600, only to discover similar quality boots for half the price at a different store. Let's say the horse world tends toward disingenuousness in general. Yes, that is a much kinder way to say: Watch out for the vultures!

While proper gear is essential, focusing on skills and passion is more important than fancy or expensive equipment.

In analyzing these unscrupulous practices, we find their allure lies within exploiting our natural inclination to trust professionals and provide the best for our children. These manipulative entities leverage this instinct against us.

Consider the case of renowned equestrian Sarah Williams. Her parents were persuaded into leasing a horse far too advanced for her level, which resulted in a debilitating fall and loss of confidence.

Points to Ponder:

Always research independently before making major financial decisions related to horseback riding.

• Check multiple sources for gear prices.

• Seek advice from independent trainers regarding suitable horses to lesson on. Seek the advice of two trainers from two different sources before you lease or buy a horse.

• Regularly reassess your child's progress and needs.

Beware! In my years observing equestrian practices, I've seen countless families fall prey to such scams. These families would describe themselves as savvy businesspeople.*

According to Equine Business Association statistics:

Awareness about potential scams can protect you from unnecessary expenses and huge disappointment.

To navigate this terrain safely:

• Do thorough research regarding costs before starting lessons.

• Be wary if anyone pushes you toward hasty buying or leasing decisions. If it is hasty, it's not a good deal for the purchaser–legit.

• Consult with independent experts when making significant choices. Paperwork always helps a lot. Read this one at least six times.

• Regularly evaluate whether your current arrangements still meet your child's evolving needs.

• Teach your child that skill development matters more than fancy equipment.

> **Remember, amidst all this complexity, the joy of seeing your child grow as an equestrian is priceless–don't let unscrupulous players dampen this joy.**

*When I arrived at Salko Farm a few years ago, the entire lesson part of the business had been in the back pocket of the self-appointed "head" instructor for several years.

The farm owner (my now husband) was oblivious to the financial embezzlement going on right under his nose. Parents said they knew the trainer was toxic, and yet their kids still rode here? This horse chick was robbing everyone blind. She even told the kids that if they ever left Salko Farm to ride anywhere else, she'd never speak to them again and they wouldn't be welcome back.

She had a rule for the other instructor, her little runaround girl, that she was not allowed to drive through the red gate at Salko Farm before *her*, the "head" instructor, on any given day. Okay, what is wrong with people? This woman was stood up at the altar and kept all the gifts and didn't send thank-yous.

Chapter 23

Horse Flipping | Auctions | Protect Yourself From Fraud

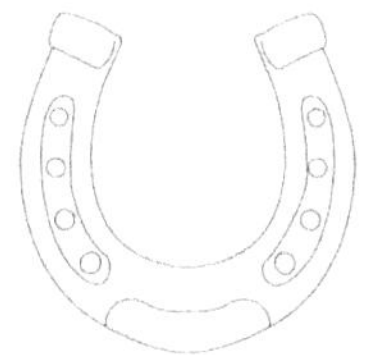

My love bug of a horse named Harley came to be mine as a result of a situation many would describe as a complete and utter disaster. Horse flipping, which involves buying horses at a low price, often "improving" them, and then reselling them for a profit, can be a controversial practice. While specific statistics on horse flipping can be hard to find due to the lack of centralized data, there are a few points worth noting that could save many horses and people from being stuck with these potentially and often unruly horses.

There has been growing concern among horse enthusiasts and animal welfare advocates regarding auctions that facilitate horse flipping. Many believe these auctions often prioritize profit over the welfare of the horses, leading to situations where animals are bought and sold without proper care or consideration for their long-term well-being.

Critics argue that the fast-paced nature of flipping can result in neglect, as flippers may prioritize quick sales rather than ensuring that horses are matched with responsible owners. This has led to calls for increased regulation of horse auctions, greater transparency, and improved support systems for both buyers and sellers.

BUT HOW? When I tried to bring a flipper to the attention of the auction site utilized to facilitate this sale, here is some of what they said:

> Since 1978, we have successfully sold 80,000 horses, generating $200 million in revenue. Based on my experience, disputes of this kind frequently lead to a cycle of mutual accusations between the parties. Buyers often allege fraud, while sellers question the actions taken by the buyer regarding the horse in question. Our responses are limited to the stipulations outlined in the contract and the evidence available to support any claims made.

Buyers have 10 days to report issues. Reserpine can last for 90 days.

Activism in this area often focuses on promoting responsible ownership, advocating for thorough vetting of buyers, and even creating alternatives to auctions that prioritize the welfare of horses. There's a movement pushing for legislation to address these issues and protect horses from being treated as mere commodities. Low-dose tranquilizer blood tests, specifically testing for reserpine, must be recorded for each and every horse exchanging hands.

I often see a particular favorite trick of the horse flippers, one of which is located in Advance, North Carolina. In my experience, on three occasions, this particular horse flipper passed along one of her project horses, describing it as drastically different from reality. This happened to me with this same seller three separate times. Every single time, it happened through the same "reputable" auction.

Some statistics indicate that many horses end up in rescue or welfare situations due to being flipped multiple times, often resulting in neglect or abandonment. According to the American Society for the Prevention of Cruelty to Animals (ASPCA), thousands of horses need rescue annually.

The most recent statistic for the number of viable horses currently living in rescues in the U.S. is 125,000. That is correct. In 2025, 125,000 horses are sane and sound and could have a home if only the businessman wouldn't choose to turn a blind eye to behavior like this, operating through a "reputable" auction.

At horse auctions, statistics show that a significant percentage of horses (sometimes over 50%) are sold for low prices, often leading to concerns about their welfare, where they actually came from, whether they have been administered a low-dose tranquilizer called reserpine, and other general concerns.

The horse industry contributes approximately $122 billion to the U.S. economy, and practices like flipping impact the overall health of horse populations and the welfare of organizations. Never mind the actual welfare of the poor unsuspecting buyer who has a crazy horse once the tranquilizer wears off. Sadly for the buyer, though, the auction "contract" they sign only gives them 10 days to discover their horse's true personality and physical reality.

There has been a push for stricter regulation in the horse-flipping market to ensure better welfare standards. Various states have enacted laws to protect horses from neglect and abuse during the flipping process.

But here is the thing, and here is what I was warned against: This is *big* business. There are *big* players in this *big* business. There is no need for the *big* business people to participate in horse flipping. This is only one part of this giant industry, and it's a part that needs to be snuffed out.

Ads will often use language like:

"Husband-safe"

"Beginner-safe"

"It's my sister's personal horse because she is going... traveling, to school, getting married, having a baby, too busy back at the kill pen paying for more horses per the pound so she and I can repeat this ungodly process over and over again..." or anything similar.

Auctions let this happen. They provide the perfect avenue to enable this type of fraud.

This is the story of only one of the three horses sold by the same "Christian," non-profit based in Advance, NC, purchased through the "reputable" auction site. I saw Maverick, now Harley, advertised for sale in early January 2025. Maverick's description went something like this: "This is my sister's personal horse, Maverick. He's beginner safe, 11 years old, and bomb-proof."

Of course, the online records have been removed, but this is how I remember it. I later discovered on the Christian Charity Instagram account that Maverick was "rescued" from a kill pen on December 3, 2024. There was a photo of him on Instagram. At this point, the whole transaction started to smell fishy. But wait, it gets better.

When I purchased Maverick and another horse from this seller in Advance, NC, in January, 2025, I was under the impression (based on the full description of these horses on the reputable auction site) that he was 11 years old (he is actually 20!), he was her sister's personal horse, and that she was so sad to be selling him—to the point that they wanted to track him and take him back if he didn't work out. Except that, when I eventually asked, it turned out not to be the case. They didn't know what I was talking about. Funny. Except it's not at all funny.

Maverick and a gray mare (also described as husband-safe and bombproof at the young age of four), arrived at Salko Farm in early February. They were both at least 200-300 pounds underweight as they stumbled off the trailer. They got off the trailer white-eyed—not a good thing to see in a horse because it means they are terrified and, most importantly, superbly dysregulated. A dysregulated horse is like a speedy tortoise. This doesn't happen easily and is not natural. A horse exists *to be* regulated. It's their job to be regulated and present. This wild-eyed look was all despite the tranquilizer these poor horses were given. I want to be super clear here. I have no proof of any of this. I do know horses, though. I also know the type of people you are likely to find infiltrating every aspect of the horse world. These people hide behind things like "Christian" charities with meaningless statistics to divert.

We've probably had more than a thousand different equines go through our new horse settling protocol since 1948, the establishment of the Salko Farm.

Every single horse is entirely different from any other horse. There are also general and similar ways that horses behave, the same as for our beloved canine pets. Having said all of that, when these two skinny horses arrived, their general ways of behaving seemed roughly in line with what we would expect, considering they had experienced the long trailer ride from Advance, NC, to Southport, CT.

They were both shockingly underweight, which was undisclosed on the auction site. Their ribs were exposed. The photos provided on the auction site were taken at the best angles to carefully conceal their skin and bone condition, and their exposed ribs.

Here is the thing, though; they were our new charity's first official rescues. Knowing it was something we had dealt with many times in the past, I figured we could do it again for these two sleepy and kind horses. They were mainly starving. I thought, *I'm a rockstar at fattening up animals.* The sleepy and kind adjectives we used for these horses, though, seemed to start wearing off a few days into their time in Connecticut.

This is when a friend mentioned the long-lasting tranquilizer drug called reserpine and how it was used to make horses seem super chill, calm, even Bob Marley-like. Hmmm 🙂—things were starting to make some pretty sick sense. I mean sick in the old-fashioned sense of the word "sick." Not the good kind of "sick."

Everything became crystal clear.

This charity was rescuing horses from kill pens and similar sales, where they pay per pound for each horse. This was step one. It may seem innocent enough... until they lie to buyers to sell them.

Step 2 is plucking an age for the rescued horse out of a hat. Not their real age, mind you, but an age that will work with the rest of the story they've created about that horse. They said Maverick (Harley) was 11 years old. He is more like 20.

Step 3 is working the horses while they're drugged and extremely underweight, another mastered skill of the typical full-time horse flipper extraordinaire.

Once I realized that I had been majorly duped by this woman, I asked the auction to ban her from using the site to facilitate these disingenuous sales. I didn't even want my money back. I wanted the madness to stop. I wanted this channel closed so people like this seller wouldn't have such an easy time passing off their QUICK FLIPS.

When I explained what I thought was going down to the auction owner, he responded with statistics about how much money they'd made since 1978. Congrats pal! The numbers he shared further proved that there may indeed be some funny business going on through his site. He told me he had been a part of over 80,000 horse sales. Then he told me he'd be lawyering up, that he stood behind the health certificate and their contracts that graciously give the buyer 10 days for the tranquilizer to wear off, enough for you to see the wildness in the beginner safe horses you've now purchased *and* paid to have hauled to the East Coast to your own farm.

We don't have any video from you regarding Pepper's rearing and bad behavior. We haven't received anything substantive to show that she has a problem or when Pepper began rearing up.

You stated that the horses have health issues yet have not provided any veterinary certificates that state that. You said they were 200 pounds underweight when you got them, but we haven't seen any photos or a vet certificate supporting that. Stating horses are drugged without any proof is a serious allegation. Without proof, it could be argued that they developed these issues since you got them.

This situation is not straightforward and does not seem to represent a clear instance of fraud, as you have not presented any evidence to support claims of fraudulent activity.

The rights and responsibility of both buyers and sellers are in the Terms of Sale (https://internethorseauctions. com/terms.php?aucid=563) which you expressly agreed to when you registered for a bidding number.

Jesse has provided information to us as we requested including health certificates dated January 23, 2025, which include photos. In light of your threats, we will forward this information to our attorney for evaluation. We will address any defamatory statements made on social media as we deem appropriate.

Maverick's bottom tooth was embedded in the roof of his mouth. His teeth had not been floated for years! It is *not* humane to exchange hands with that one existing neglectful condition. That was only the beginning for poor Maverick. He had been worked steadily for 30 days. From kill pen to *beginner-safe,* while tragically thin. He still gets lippy about treats because he was so starved when he got to us in Connecticut, and had been starving for a very long time.

The Christian Charity similarly described Pepper. Her feet *would not stay on the ground* once the tranq wore off. She reared and bucked all day long or whenever a male person went near her. I'm not sure what goes on in NC, but where I come from, that is a green horse. An unbroken horse. A young and very dangerous horse. The seller knew that we operate a lesson barn and understood that we needed beginner-safe horses for that program. She swore up and down that both of these horses would be *perfect*. They are both puppy dogs, she said. Beginner-safe horses, she said.

Pepper was taken to Massachusetts to be retrained and is now with her own little girl. Our friend in MA put in the time to build up her health and strength, and trained her to keep her feet on the ground, to be steady, etc. It was not safe to have her on our property. The training and time put into her cost us $1,500, after paying $4,600 plus shipping for Pepper in the first instance.

Our costs included:

- Maverick (renamed Harley): $4,000.
- Shipping: $650 each horse.
- Equine Dentist: $700.
- Re-training: $8,750* + $4,600 = $18,700. It cost us nearly $20,000 to end up with *one* horse that is a great therapy horse and will be able to be ridden on the trails.

It took us from April to August to train and board (another $1,750 per month) to find the original insides of that horse without all the trauma and dysregulation.

He needed magnawave and other therapies to get his dysregulated state under control. To get him less human-like and more horse-like.

Do you see how this game these people play does not end well for horses? More times than not, they end up back in a rescue situation, or worse.

Harley is now the perfect horse to assist me in my work with the residents of a rehab house for men with histories of substance abuse. Harley, Ginger, and I go onto the property every week. We host groups and one-on-one Equine Gestalt™ sessions. The lives of the men are changing as fresh perspectives become available to them when old self-limiting beliefs are cleared away.

I assure you that steps are being taken to put an end to this sort of practice. Watch this space! I have a story sitting on hold with a major network that is considering a mini-series on this subject as a way to expose and address some inhumane acts. Check out www.somatice quineexperiences.org for more information on Harley, Ginger, GiGi, and the others we are in the process of rescuing from 13 Hands Rescue in Clinton Corners, NY. Two more minis are coming to Salko Farm this fall: Toby & Talulla!

Chapter 24

Conclusion

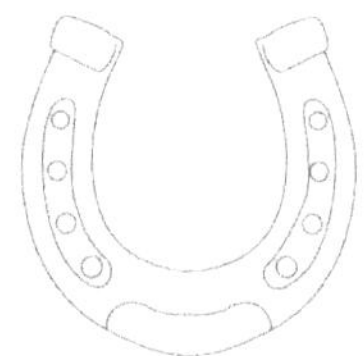

This book began as a small reference booklet for the parents of our riders here at Salko Farm. As the chapters unfolded, it took on a life of its own.

This book has covered everything from equestrian-specific exercises for humans wanting to strengthen their riding muscles to purchasing your first horse.

Most importantly for me, it will ensure that as many humans as possible understand the benefit of having horses in their lives and the lives of their children.

HORSE =

Be. Here. Now.

Authenticity. What you see is what you get.

Responsibility.

Focus.

Attentiveness.

Compassion.

Vulnerability.

Presence.

Contact.

Lie detector.

Best friend.

Confidente.

So much more than just a bike!

We've talked about how important grooming is for the horse to bond with his human before he allows that predator onto his back, the importance of choosing the right barn–riding instructors, the size of horses, and the moxie required to handle them can be difficult to navigate.

I highly recommend that you involve someone you trust if you venture into equine ownership. If you have no one to trust, either email us and we will point you toward a reputable horseperson in a state near you or re-read Chapter 16 on equine purchases.

Where will you board this horse? Do you know a barn owner you trust to look after your horse well and are you willing to play nicely with all riders/boarders at the barn? An organized whiteboard and tidy aisles in the barns are an excellent place to start regarding initial findings at any riding establishment. Disorganized chaos, mismanaged tack lying around, and dirty water buckets are not signs of a primo-riding barn. Don't let chandeliers fool you, however; they don't necessarily mean all is rosy, sweet, and filled with beautiful light.

The horse world is a place to always keep your wits about you. Not only do you want to continue your diligence with making sure you are not stepped on by any of the 1,200-pound toddlers you may encounter in your lifetime, but you also want to pay close attention to the certifications and overall vibe you discover at any potential barn. This is paramount. The situation I found at Salko Farm when I arrived quite a few years back was sketchy beyond anything I had ever encountered. The self-appointed "head" instructor in charge of the entire business was embezzling money from parents and brainwashing the young girls. She had favorites and pitted the girls against each other frequently. Elaborate stories were fabricated and then delivered around the farm as fact. One of her fantasies had me pregnant with twins (I was 53 with tied tubes!), running from the Canadian government, and poisoning my new husband, Chris.

GET A FEELING FOR THE VIBE OF THE BARN... pay attention to your gut instincts.

You have uncovered different riding styles and received a deeper explanation of the fastest-growing equestrian sport, Working Equitation.

Every rider is different and comes from a different background and level of strength. Riders also start at all different ages, from between two and three years old. You may begin your riding journey at Salko Farm at the age of three. The time it takes to learn any skill with a horse is anyone's guess. In my opinion, the best instructor is the one who takes the longest before the child canters. There is so much to learn about body positioning and staying in the center of the horse. Strength within specific muscle groups is also required before cantering is safe. Kids must also know their left from their right if riding in a ring with others.

Equine Gestalt™ and horses healing humans in general through any Equine Assisted Service are my biggest passions within this pretty awesome book! Words can't describe how my life has changed because of these magical creatures and their healing effects. It is so important for me to share this with as many humans as possible. Spending time near horses will change your life for the better–well, unless you are the one paying for said horses… In that case, you will find your life changed for the better when you see the smiles on the faces of your loved ones riding said horses.

As I said, you can always put the book down if you get tired of my jokes.

From your first ride to your first purchase, we hope this book has covered the most important bases for a smooth experience.

Bibliography

13 Hands Rescue, Clinton Corners, New York
https://13handsequine.org/

Touched By a Horse, Chase, British Columbia
https://touchedbyahorse.com/